DISCARD
Porter County
Library System

Introductory College Grammar and Writing

D1567172

Valparaiso Public Library
103 Jefferson Street
Valparaiso, IN 46383

DISCARD
Porter County
Library System

Introductory College Grammar and Writing

Practical Grammar for Developing Writers

Marian Anders

ALAMANCE COMMUNITY COLLEGE

PORTER COUNTY LIBRARY

Valparaiso Public Library
103 Jefferson Street
Valparaiso, IN 46383

CAROLINA ACADEMIC PRESS

Durham, North Carolina

NF   428.2 AND   VAL
Anders, Marian.
Introductory college grammar a
33410011258987
            SEP 1 3 2011

Copyright © 2011
Marian Anders
All Rights Reserved

Library of Congress Cataloging-in-Publication Data

Anders, Marian.
 Introductory college grammar and writing : practical grammar for developing writers / Marian Anders.
   p. cm.
 ISBN 978-1-61163-060-2 (alk. paper)
 1. English language--Grammar. 2. English language--Rhetoric. I. Title.

PE1112.A53 2011
428.2--dc23

                         2011018887

Carolina Academic Press
700 Kent Street
Durham, North Carolina 27701
Telephone (919) 489-7486
Fax (919) 493-5668
www.cap-press.com

Printed in the United States of America

Contents

Quick Reference Page

A **clause** is a group of words that has a subject and a verb.

A **phrase** is a group of words that doesn't have a subject and a verb.

An **independent clause** sounds finished.

A **dependent clause** has a subordinating conjunction, so it doesn't sound finished.

A **simple sentence** has only one clause, an independent clause.

A **compound sentence** has two independent clauses.

A **complex sentence** as one independent clause and a dependent clause.

A **fragment** is a sentence that doesn't have an independent clause.

A **comma splice** is a sentence that has two independent clauses with only a comma between them.

A **run-on** is a sentence that has two independent clauses with nothing between them.

There are three methods for fixing a comma splice or run-on:

1) semi-colon (;)
2) comma with a coordinating conjunction (, and)
3) subordinating conjunction (After)

Coordinating Conjunctions — FANBOYS

for, and, nor, but, or, yet, so

Common Subordinating Conjunctions

after	although	as	because	before
if	since	so that	that	though
till/until	unless	when	where	while

Introductory College Grammar and Writing

Chapter 1

Verbs

To find the verb in a sentence, change the tense (or time) of the sentence by saying *yesterday, every day,* and *tomorrow* at the beginning of the sentence. When you put those three words at the beginning of the sentence, you are changing the tense or the time when the sentence happened. When you change the tense, the verb will change automatically. Notice that every word in all three sentences is exactly the same except for the verb.

Yesterday   Steve **ate** pizza. (past tense)

Every day   Steve **eats** pizza. (present tense)

Tomorrow   Steve **will eat** pizza. (future tense)

People often have a hard time finding the verb when they LOOK for the verb. Instead, change the tense and LISTEN for the word that changes.

Yesterday   Jill **bought** a new pair of shoes. (past tense)

Every day   Jill **buys** a new pair of shoes. (present tense)

Tomorrow   Jill **will buy** a new pair of shoes. (future tense)

Try these on your own and then turn the page to check your answers.

My dog bites the newspaper delivery boy.

Yesterday   My dog . . .

Every day   My dog . . .

Tomorrow   My dog . . .

Did you notice that the "every day" sentence is the same as the original sentence? That's because the original sentence was written in present tense. The verb changes when you CHANGE the tense, which is why we need three different time words. One of them won't change anything, but the other two will.

George hit a home run.

Yesterday   George . . .

Every day   George . . .

Tomorrow   George . . .

Here are the answers:

Yesterday   My dog **bit** the pizza delivery man.

Every day   My dog **bites** the pizza delivery man.

Tomorrow   My dog **will bite** the pizza delivery man.

Yesterday   George **hit** a home run.

Every day   George **hits** a home run.

Tomorrow   George **will hit** a home run.

Let's try some tricky sentences. Remember, don't LOOK for the verb. LISTEN for the word that changes.

Jackie loves baking brownies.

Yesterday   Jackie **loved** baking brownies. (past tense)

Every day   Jackie **loves** baking brownies. (present tense)

Tomorrow   Jackie **will love** baking brownies. (future tense)

Are you surprised that BAKING wasn't the verb? Many of us have been taught that the verb is the action word, and sometimes that's true, but not always. The verb is the word that changes when you change the tense.

Try these on your own and then check your answers on the next page:

Susan went to the mall to go shopping.

Yesterday   Susan . . .

Every day   Susan . . .

Tomorrow   Susan . . .

Mark wants to win the Heisman trophy.

Yesterday   Mark . . .

Every day   Mark . . .

Tomorrow   Mark . . .

Here are the answers:

Yesterday   Susan **went** to the mall to go shopping.

Every day   Susan **goes** to the mall to go shopping.

Tomorrow   Susan **will go** to the mall to go shopping.

Yesterday   Mark **wanted** to win the Heisman trophy.

Every day   Mark **wants** to win the Heisman trophy.

Tomorrow   Mark **will want** to win the Heisman trophy.

These sentences were tricky. Don't be discouraged if you had some trouble. Just keep using your ears rather than your eyes, and with practice you will be able to find the verb easily.

Sometimes you may wonder how many words to mark for the verb. You already know that in future tense (*Tomorrow . . .*) the verb is two words. Sometimes the verb can even be three (or four!) words working together. How do you know how many words to mark?

Mark the word that changes when you change the time. Then look right next to that word and see if there are any more words that seem to be working with the word you marked. Mark them too.

Joe **drinks** lemonade.

Joe **will drink** lemonade.

Joe **has been drinking** lemonade.

Joe **has drunk** three glasses of lemonade.

The good news is that for practical grammar, it really doesn't matter if you mark every verb word. What matters is that you can tell if there is a verb in the sentence.

Compound Verbs

A sentence can have more than one verb. This is called a COMPOUND verb. When you change the tense, ALL the verbs in the sentence will change.

Jack mows the grass and trims the shrubs.

Yesterday   Jack **mowed** the grass and **trimmed** the shrubs. (past tense)

Every day   Jack **mows** the grass and **trims** the shrubs. (present tense)

Tomorrow   Jack **will mow** the grass and **trim** the shrubs. (future tense)

After dinner Gloria washed the dishes, and Bob dried them.

Yesterday   After dinner Gloria **washed** the dishes, and Bob **dried** them. (past)

Every day   After dinner Gloria **washes** the dishes, and Bob **dries** them. (present)

Tomorrow   After dinner Gloria **will wash** the dishes, and Bob **will dry** them. (future)

The garden will look beautiful and will smell heavenly.

Yesterday   The garden **looked** beautiful and **smelled** heavenly. (past tense)

Every day   The garden **looks** beautiful and **smells** heavenly. (present tense)

Tomorrow   The garden **will look** beautiful and **will smell** heavenly. (future tense)

EXERCISE 1.1 — Finding Verbs

Say *yesterday*, *every day*, and *tomorrow* at the beginning of each sentence and listen for the words that change. Some sentences have one verb, and others have two. Mark the verbs with a <u>double underline</u>.

1. My brother lives in Florida.

2. He has an apartment just two blocks from the beach.

3. I visited him last summer.

4. We fished off the pier and caught three snook.

5. The pelicans watched us; they wanted a handout.

6. The sun was hot, and I got a sunburn.

7. When we went back to the apartment, we went for a swim in the pool.

8. I was as red as a lobster.

9. My brother and I had a great time together.

10. I will go back to Florida for my next vacation.

EXERCISE 1.2 — Finding Verbs

Say *yesterday*, *every day*, and *tomorrow* at the beginning of each sentence and listen for the words that change. Some sentences have one verb, and others have two. Mark the verbs with a <u>double underline</u>.

1. George loves gardening.

2. He works in his yard every weekend.

3. George went on-line and ordered six apple trees.

4. The trees came in the mail in a big cardboard box; they were only three feet tall.

5. George got very sweaty when he dug six holes in his yard.

6. He dug large holes and got blisters on his hands.

7. Then he put compost and fertilizer in each hole.

8. He planted the trees and firmed the soil around their roots.

9. Now the little trees are blooming, and the blossoms look so pretty.

10. In four years, George will harvest his first apples.

EXERCISE 1.3 — Finding Verbs

Say yesterday, every day, and tomorrow at the beginning of each sentence and listen for the words that change. Some sentences have one verb, and others have two. Mark the verbs with a <u>double underline</u>.

1. The leaves on the rose bush were drooping.

2. George lifted a leaf and turned it over.

3. He saw a dozen aphids.

4. Aphids are plant vampires; they suck the plant's juices.

5. As they drink the plant juices, aphids produce a sweet liquid called honeydew.

6. Honeydew is delicious to ants.

7. Ants actually farm aphids for their honeydew just like people farm cows for milk.

8. With his thumb, George squished the aphids and killed them.

9. The ants went crazy; they ran all over the rose bush trying to save their aphids

10. George cared more about saving his rose bush.

Chapter 2

Subjects

Finding the Subject

Anytime you analyze a sentence, always find the verb first. Then you can do the second step: find the subject by asking yourself, *"who or what did the verb?"*

> Brittany baked some fudge brownies.

Tomorrow   Brittany **will bake** some fudge brownies.

Every day   Brittany **bakes** some fudge brownies.

The word that changed when I changed the tense was BAKED, so BAKED is the verb. Now, to find the subject ask yourself, *"Who or what did the verb?"* Say *"who or what"* and then say the verb and read the rest of the sentence to the end.

> *Who or what* **baked** some fudge brownies?

The answer, of course, is BRITTANY. Mark the subject with a single underline.

> <u>Brittany</u> <u>baked</u> some fudge brownies.

Were you tempted to say that BROWNIES was the subject? Ask yourself, "Did the brownies bake anything?" No, Brittany baked them, so the subject is <u>Brittany</u>.

In most of the sentences we write in English, the subject of the sentence comes before the verb. In some tricky sentences, the subject can come after the verb, but that doesn't happen too often. So look in front of the verb to find the subject.

EXERCISE 2.1 — Finding the Subject

Use the three time words *yesterday, every day,* and *tomorrow* to find the verb. <u>Double underline</u> the verb. Then ask *"who or what did the verb?"* to find the subject. Mark the subject by <u>underlining</u> it.

EXAMPLE:

(Find the Verb) The weather forecast <u>called</u> for rain.

(Ask) *Who or what called for rain?*

(Underline) The weather <u>forecast</u> <u>called</u> for rain.

1. (Find the Verb) The sky was dark.

    (Ask) *Who or what was dark?*

    (Underline) The sky was dark.

2. (Find the Verb) Thunder boomed in the distance.

    (Ask) *Who or what boomed in the distance?*

    (Underline) Thunder boomed in the distance.

3. (Find the Verb) Lightning flashed through the sky.

    (Ask) *Who or what flashed through the sky?*

    (Underline) Lightning flashed through the sky.

4. (Find the Verb) Raindrops pounded onto the roof.

    (Ask) *Who or what pounded onto the roof?*

    (Underline) Raindrops pounded onto the roof.

5. (Find the Verb) The dog hid under the bed.

    (Ask) *Who or what hid under the bed?*

    (Underline) The dog hid under the bed.

EXERCISE 2.2 — Finding the Subject

Use the three time words *yesterday, every day,* and *tomorrow* to find the verb. <u>Double underline</u> the verb. Then ask *"who or what did the verb?"* to find the subject. Mark the subject by <u>underlining</u> it.

EXAMPLE: <u>Jamal</u> <u>is</u> a wide receiver on the Falcon football team.

1. Jamal averages fourteen points per game.

2. He has direct focus and great hands.

3. He is also very fast.

4. Jamal ran for eighty yards in the game last weekend.

5. In the third quarter, he caught an interception.

6. The fans cheered!

7. The other team snarled with anger.

8. Jamal drank Gatorade on the sidelines.

9. He wanted to stay hydrated.

10. The Falcons won the game by twenty-one points.

EXERCISE 2.3 — Finding the Subject

Use the three time words *yesterday, every day,* and *tomorrow* to find the verb. <u>Double underline</u> the verb. Then ask *"who or what did the verb?"* to find the subject. Mark the subject by <u>underlining</u> it.

1. Chandra took her niece to the circus.

2. The auditorium was really crowded.

3. Chandra bought some pink and blue cotton candy.

4. A lady walked on a tightrope.

5. Tigers jumped through hoops of fire.

6. A clown juggled five rings.

7. A trapeze artist swung by his legs.

8. Ten elephants walked in a circle.

9. The master of ceremonies wore a bright blue tuxedo.

10. Chandra's niece had a lot of fun.

Compound Subjects

Sometimes a sentence can have more than one subject. Two people may be doing something together. This is called a COMPOUND SUBJECT.

> Katie and Jake <u>swim</u> at the YMCA.

The verb is SWIM. To find the subject, ask yourself *"Who swims at the YMCA?"* Katie and Jake both swim. They are two subjects sharing one verb, so underline both names, like this:

> <u>Katie</u> and <u>Jake</u> <u>swim</u> at the YMCA.

Picky Stuff: Notice that I did not underline the word AND. AND is not a subject. Would you say "And swims at the YMCA"? No.

> <u>Katie</u> <u>swims</u> at the YMCA.   *That sounds fine.*
>
> <u>And</u> <u>swims</u> at the YMCA.   *That sounds like somebody is named AND!*
>
> <u>Jake</u> <u>swims</u> at the YMCA   *That sounds fine.*

EXERCISE 2.4 — Compound Subjects

Use the three time words *yesterday, every day,* and *tomorrow* to find the verb. <u>Double underline</u> the verb. Then ask *"who or what did the verb?"* to find the subject. Mark the subject by <u>underlining</u> it.

1. Mosquitoes and fleas made our camping trip miserable.

2. Joe and Jim are allergic to animal fur.

3. Cats and dogs make them sneeze.

4. Christmas and Easter are my favorite holidays.

5. Mom or Dad will call me tonight.

One Word Subjects

You might wonder how many words to underline for each subject. Sometimes you need to underline two or three words, but usually it's best to underline only one word. Look at these examples:

> My brother <u>is</u> thirteen years old.

Who or what is thirteen years old? MY BROTHER. Ok, that's right, but if you want to underline only ONE word, which word would you choose? BROTHER is a better choice than MY, so just underline BROTHER.

Here's another example:

> Jessica's room <u>is</u> really messy.

Who or what is really messy? JESSICA'S ROOM. Which one word would you choose? Is JESSICA really messy? (Maybe she is, but that's not what the sentence is about.) Is the ROOM really messy? Yes. ROOM is the best choice.

Now here is a really tricky one!

> My favorite ride at Disney World <u>is</u> the Haunted Mansion.

Who or what is the Haunted Mansion? DISNEY WORLD is the Haunted Mansion? That doesn't sound right. How about MY FAVORITE RIDE is the Haunted Mansion? That sounds good, but it's three words. Which ONE word would you choose? RIDE is the best choice.

EXERCISE 2.5 — One Word Subjects

Use the three time words *yesterday, every day,* and *tomorrow* to find the verb. <u>Double underline</u> the verb. Then ask *"who or what did the verb?"* to find the subject. Mark just one word by <u>underlining</u> it.

EXAMPLE: My new <u>pet</u> <u>is</u> a garter snake.

1. Chrystal's new haircut is too short.

2. The team's star quarterback hurt his knee.

3. The book's paper cover was torn.

4. All three pink and purple striped lollipops fell in the mud.

5. My favorite pink polka-dotted satin prom gown costs $250.

Strange Subjects

In Chapter 1 you learned to find verbs by listening for the word that changes rather than by looking with your eyes. A word may LOOK like a verb, but if it doesn't change when we change the tense, it's not doing the job of a verb in that sentence.

> Jackie <u>loves</u> baking brownies.

The word BAKING looks like it would be the verb, but it doesn't change when we change the time. The real verb is LOVES.

Sometimes a word that looks like a verb can actually be the subject of a sentence.

> <u>Dancing</u> <u>is</u> fun.

> <u>Washing</u> the dishes <u>is</u> not fun.

So don't get confused if the answer to your subject question *Who or what did the verb?* happens to be a word that looks like a verb. In grammar, it doesn't matter what a word looks like. What matters is the JOB it is doing in the sentence.

EXERCISE 2.6 — Strange Subjects

<u>Double underline</u> the verb. Then ask *"who or what did the verb?"* to find the subject. Mark the subject by <u>underlining</u> it.

     EXAMPLE: <u>Watching</u> TV <u>is</u> very relaxing.

1. Gardening is my favorite hobby.

2. Hitchhiking is dangerous.

3. Acting on Broadway was Trisha's dream.

4. Eating crackers in bed is messy.

5. Sleeping on the ground is uncomfortable.

Chapter 3

Clauses and Phrases

A CLAUSE is a group of words that has a subject and a verb. A PHRASE is a group of words that doesn't have a subject and a verb. We put clauses and phrases together to make sentences of different lengths. A very short sentence would have just one clause. A very long sentence could have several clauses and several phrases.

How to Tell if a Group of Words Is a Clause

First change the tense and listen for a word that changes:

Lucy is four years old

Yesterday   Lucy **was** four years old

Every day   Lucy **is** four years old

Tomorrow   Lucy **will be** four years old

The word IS changed, so we found a verb. Now we'll ask *"who or what is four years old?"* The answer is LUCY, so that's the subject.

Lucy <u>is</u> four years old

This group of words has a verb and a subject, so it is a clause.

Let's try another one:

My sister's baby

Yesterday   My sister's baby

Everyday   My sister's baby

Tomorrow   My sister's baby

We tried all three tenses, but nothing changed. That's because this group of words does not have a verb. A verb will always change when you change the time. Nothing changed, so there's no verb here.

A clause needs A VERB AND A SUBJECT. Since there's no verb, we don't even have to worry about trying to find a subject. We can tell right away that this group of words is not a clause. It's a phrase.

A phrase might have a verb but no subject, or it might have a subject but no verb, or it might not have either one:

> Loves her teddy bear (verb but no subject)
>
> My sister's baby (subject but no verb)
>
> After her nap (neither one!)

EXERCISE 3.1 — Clauses and Phrases

Double underline the verbs and underline the subjects. If a group of words has a subject and a verb, circle CLAUSE. If it is missing something, circle PHRASE.

EXAMPLE:	Lucy is my niece	(CLAUSE)	PHRASE
1.	She watches *Sesame Street*	CLAUSE	PHRASE
2.	Knows all the muppets	CLAUSE	PHRASE
3.	Elmo is her favorite	CLAUSE	PHRASE
4.	This year for Halloween	CLAUSE	PHRASE
5.	She wants an Elmo costume	CLAUSE	PHRASE
6.	Lucy is learning the ABCs	CLAUSE	PHRASE
7.	And also learning to count	CLAUSE	PHRASE
8.	She threw cookies	CLAUSE	PHRASE
9.	In the air like Cookie Monster	CLAUSE	PHRASE
10.	Made a big mess	CLAUSE	PHRASE

EXERCISE 3.2 — Clauses and Phrases

Double underline the verbs and underline the subjects. If a group of words has a subject and a verb, circle CLAUSE. If it is missing something, circle PHRASE.

EXAMPLE:	Four thousand years ago	CLAUSE	(PHRASE)

1.	Egyptians made mummies	CLAUSE	PHRASE
2.	Not only of dead people	CLAUSE	PHRASE
3.	But also of their pets	CLAUSE	PHRASE
4.	Archaeologists found mummies	CLAUSE	PHRASE
5.	Of cats, dogs, birds, and even crocodiles	CLAUSE	PHRASE
6.	The Egyptians removed the inner organs	CLAUSE	PHRASE
7.	Then wrapped the animal's body	CLAUSE	PHRASE
8.	In linen bandages	CLAUSE	PHRASE
9.	This process took seventy days	CLAUSE	PHRASE
10.	Ancient Egyptians really loved their pets	CLAUSE	PHRASE

Prepositional Phrases

As you know, a phrase is a group of words that doesn't have a subject and a verb. In **traditional** grammar, there are MANY different names for different kinds of phrases based on what job the phrase is doing in a sentence.

In **practical** grammar, it really doesn't matter what job a phrase is doing. For analyzing sentences and writing correctly, a phrase is a phrase, and that's all that matters. But there is one particular kind of phrase that is good to know because we use it all the time in speaking and writing: the prepositional phrase.

A preposition is a word that tells what a cat can do with a chair.

A cat can be   IN the chair
                UNDER the chair
                BENEATH the chair
                ON TOP OF the chair
                BESIDE the chair
                NEAR the chair
                BY the chair
                WITH the chair

A cat can jump   OVER the chair
                ON the chair
                INTO the chair
                OFF the chair
                FROM the chair

A cat can run   AROUND the chair
                PAST the chair
                TO the chair
                THROUGH the legs of the chair

A cat can sit so still that it looks like part   OF the chair

A **prepositional phrase** is a group of words that starts with a preposition and then has a couple more words that complete the idea.

There is one practical reason for learning prepositional phrases: the subject or verb of a sentence will NEVER be inside a prepositional phrase. So if you have a really long sentence, you could first put parentheses around all the prepositional phrases. Then just look at the words you have left over to find the subject and verb.

The <u>cat</u> <u>ran</u> (around the chair) and <u>jumped</u> (into my lap).

EXERCISE 3.3 — Prepositional Phrases

Draw parentheses around the prepositional phrases in these sentences. <u>Double underline</u> the verbs and <u>underline</u> the subjects. One of these sentences has a compound verb.

> EXAMPLE: <u>Alligators</u> <u>live</u> (in swamps) (in Florida.)

1. Alligators swim through the water in the swamps.

2. Only the alligator's eyes are above the surface of the water.

3. Seagulls fly over the palm trees.

4. Near the shore, egrets walk on the sand.

5. Under the water, fish swim around the water plants.

6. A turtle suns himself on top of a fallen log.

7. The turtle steps off the log and hits the water with a splash.

8. Mosquitoes buzz in the tall grass.

9. Water snakes glide on the surface of the water.

10. A frog jumps from a rock to a log and into the water.

Chapter 4

Sentence Types Part 1 — Simple and Compound

Phrases and clauses are the building blocks that we use to make different kinds of sentences. A short sentence has only one clause. A long sentence can have many clauses and phrases.

EXERCISE 4.1 — Labeling Clauses

Some of these sentences have one clause, and some of them have two clauses. Follow the steps to analyze each sentence:

Step 1: Use the three time words (*yesterday, every day, tomorrow*) to find the verbs. Double underline the <u>verbs</u>.

Step 2: Ask *"who or what did the verb?"* to find the subjects. Underline the <u>subjects</u>.

Step 3: Write **Clause** or C under each clause. You don't need to write anything under the phrases.

Step 4: Count how many clauses are in each sentence.

EXAMPLE: <u>James</u> <u>got</u> some free tickets, so <u>he</u> <u>went</u> to a Bulls baseball game.
          Clause   Clause

1.   The Durham Bulls played a great game.

2.   Their first batter hit a home run, and the crowd cheered.

3.   The Bulls' pitcher struck out most of the batters.

4.   The other team made some hits, but the Bulls' center fielder caught them.

5.   The Bulls won the game seven to zero.

A SIMPLE SENTENCE has one clause.

> <u>Josephine</u> <u>wore</u> a purple velvet gown.
>   C

> (At the New Year's Eve Ball), <u>Josephine</u> <u>wore</u> a purple velvet gown (with a satin cape).
>   C

The second sentence is much longer because it has two phrases. But it is still a simple sentence because it still has only one clause. When we analyze sentence type, phrases don't matter; all that matters is clauses.

A COMPOUND sentence has two clauses.

> <u>Philip</u> <u>saw</u> Josephine; <u>he</u> <u>asked</u> her to dance.
>   C   C

> <u>Philip</u> <u>saw</u> Josephine (across the ballroom); (with a nervous voice) <u>he</u> <u>asked</u> her to dance.
>   C   C

The second sentence is much longer because it has two phrases, but it is still a compound sentence because it has two clauses. Phrases don't matter.

EXERCISE 4.2 — Simple and Compound Sentences

Follow the steps to analyze each sentence.

Step 1: Use the three time words (*yesterday, every day, tomorrow*) to find the verbs. Double underline the verbs.

Step 2: Ask *"who or what did the verb?"* to find the subjects. Underline the subjects.

Step 3: Write **Clause** or **C** under each clause.

Step 4: Count the clauses. If the sentence has one clause, circle **S** for Simple. If the sentence has two clauses, circle **CP** for Compound.

EXAMPLE: Mark went to the basketball game; he sat near the cheerleaders.   S   (CP)
                   C   C

1. Mark watched Cassie cheer, but Cassie ignored Mark.   S   CP

2. The basketball game was exciting and intense.   S   CP

3. Mark didn't watch the game; he was in love with Cassie.   S   CP

4. At halftime, the cheerleaders took a break.   S   CP

5. Cassie waved at Mark, and Mark turned bright red with embarrassment.   S   CP

EXERCISE 4.3 — Simple and Compound Sentences

Follow the steps to analyze each sentence.

Step 1: Use the three time words (*yesterday, every day, tomorrow*) to find the verbs. Double underline the <u>verbs</u>.

Step 2: Ask *"who or what did the verb?"* to find the subjects. Underline the <u>subjects</u>.

Step 3: Write **Clause** or **C** under each clause.

Step 4: Count the clauses. If the sentence has one clause, circle **S** for Simple. If the sentence has two clauses, circle **CP** for Compound.

EXAMPLE: <u>People</u> <u>use</u> pennies all the time, but <u>we</u> <u>don't</u> look at them too often.   S   (CP)
          C   C

1. Pennies are made from copper.	S	CP
2. Abraham Lincoln's face is on the front of the penny.	S	CP
3. The front also has a date; the date tells the age of the penny.	S	CP
4. The back side shows the Lincoln Memorial.	S	CP
5. The back also says "E Pluribus Unum."	S	CP
6. "E Pluribus Unum" is Latin for "from many, one."	S	CP
7. The Roman poet Virgil wrote this phrase, and it appears on all U.S. coins.	S	CP
8. The word "many" refers to the thirteen colonies.	S	CP
9. The word "one" means one nation, the United States of America.	S	CP
10. The thirteen colonies joined together, and they formed one nation.	S	CP

EXERCISE 4.4 — Simple and Compound Sentences

Follow the steps to analyze each sentence.

Step 1: Use the three time words (*yesterday, every day, tomorrow*) to find the verbs. Double underline the <u>verbs</u>.

Step 2: Ask *"who or what did the verb?"* to find the subjects. Underline the <u>subjects</u>.

Step 3: Write **Clause** or **C** under each clause.

Step 4: Count the clauses. If the sentence has one clause, circle **S** for Simple. If the sentence has two clauses, circle **CP** for Compound.

EXAMPLE: The first coffee <u>plants</u> <u>grew</u> wild in Ethiopia.   (S)   CP
                          C

1. The plants spread to Arabia; Arabs started using coffee around 900 A.D.   S   CP

2. Arabs used coffee for medicine and for religious ceremonies.   S   CP

3. European ships sailed to Arabia, and the sailors traded for coffee.   S   CP

4. The ships brought coffee to Rome.   S   CP

5. Catholic priests distrusted coffee, but the Pope was curious.   S   CP

6. He smelled the drink, and then he took a sip.   S   CP

7. The Pope declared coffee delicious.   S   CP

8. Coffee spread throughout Europe.   S   CP

9. In England and America, tea was more popular than coffee for many years.   S   CP

10. King George put a tax on tea, so people started drinking coffee instead.   S   CP

Chapter 5

Independent and Dependent Clauses

You already know that a clause is a group of words that has a subject and a verb. Now we are going to learn the two different kinds of clauses: independent clauses and dependent clauses. Both kinds of clauses have a subject and a verb. The difference between them is that a dependent clause also has an extra word at the beginning. This extra word is called a **subordinating conjunction**.

Subordinating Conjunctions

Think of some words that begin with the prefix SUB.

submarine   subway   sub-flooring

These are all things that go underneath or below something else. The submarine goes under the water; the subway goes under the street; the sub-flooring is the layer of plywood that goes under the carpet.

subordinate   subservient   submissive

These words describe someone who is not powerful. In the military, soldiers must do what their commander says. The soldiers are subordinate to the commander. The same is true in the workplace. The boss tells her subordinates what to do. A person who is subservient or submissive willingly obeys another person.

So the prefix SUB means beneath, below, less powerful. A **subordinating conjunction** is a word that goes at the beginning of a clause and makes a clause less powerful.

Common Subordinating Conjunctions				
after	although	as	because	before
if	since	so that	that	though
till/until	unless	when	where	while

Subordinating Conjunctions and Dependent Clauses

Subordinating conjunctions are very powerful words. When you put one of them at the beginning of a clause, the clause sounds different.

> Jose ate dinner

This is a clause, right? It has a subject and a verb. Say the clause out loud and listen to how your voice sounds. Do you sound like you're finished? Jose ate dinner.

Yes. When you get to the end, it sounds like you're finished.

Notice what happens when you put a subordinating conjunction at the beginning of the clause:

> AFTER Jose ate dinner . . .

The subject and the verb are still there, so it's still a clause. But notice how the word AFTER changes the way your voice sounds when you say this clause.

> After Jose ate dinner . . .

Now it doesn't sound like you're finished anymore. We are expecting to hear WHAT HAPPENED after Jose ate dinner. Did he watch TV? Did he wash the dishes? What happened?

A **Subordinating Conjunction** is a word that goes at the beginning of a clause. It changes the sound of the clause to make the reader want to know what happened next. Mark subordinating conjunctions with a wavy underline.

A **Dependent Clause** is a clause that starts with a subordinating conjunction. It still has a subject and a verb, but it does not sound complete. It leaves the reader asking "what happened next?"

An **Independent Clause** does not have a subordinating conjunction. It sounds complete.

> After Jose ate dinner, he washed the dishes.
>
> Dependent clause   Independent clause

The dependent clause depends on the second (independent) clause to finish the idea.

EXERCISE 5.1 — Subordinating Conjunctions

Write a different subordinating conjunction on each of the wavy underlines. Then write a second (independent) clause to finish the idea. Mark the verbs and subjects in the clauses you write.

EXAMPLE: When Jake washed his car, he was very careful.

～～～～～～ Jake washed his car,

～～～～～～ Jake washed his car,

～～～～～～ Jake washed his car,

～～～～～～ Jake washed his car,

～～～～～～ Jake washed his car,

Common Subordinating Conjunctions				
after	although	as	because	before
if	since	so that	that	though
till/until	unless	when	where	while

EXERCISE 5.2 — Independent and Dependent Clauses

Step 1: Double underline the <u>verbs</u> and underline the subjects.

Step 2: Look at the first word of the clause to see if it is a subordinating conjunction. If you find a subordinating conjunction, mark it with a wavy underline.

Step 3: If the clause has a subordinating conjunction, circle DEPENDENT. If it does not have a subordinating conjunction, circle INDEPENDENT.

EXAMPLE: I hate mosquitos   Dependent   (Independent)

1. Since they bite me   Dependent   Independent

2. I try to kill them   Dependent   Independent

3. When I am outside   Dependent   Independent

4. Mosquitoes drive me crazy   Dependent   Independent

5. While I mow the grass   Dependent   Independent

6. I can't swat them   Dependent   Independent

7. Because I have to push the mower   Dependent   Independent

8. Before I go outside   Dependent   Independent

9. I put on bug repellent cream   Dependent   Independent

10. The cream keeps mosquitoes away   Dependent   Independent

EXERCISE 5.3 — Independent and Dependent Clauses

Step 1: Double underline the <u>verbs</u> and underline the <u>subjects</u>.

Step 2: Look at the first word of the clause to see if it is a subordinating conjunction. If you find a subordinating conjunction, mark it with a <u>wavy underline</u>.

Step 3: If the clause has a subordinating conjunction, circle DEPENDENT. If it does not have a subordinating conjunction, circle INDEPENDENT.

EXAMPLE: <u>Fall</u> <u>is</u> my favorite season.   Dependent   (Independent)

1. A big maple tree is in my front yard   Dependent   Independent

2. When the weather turns cool   Dependent   Independent

3. The leaves turn bright orange   Dependent   Independent

4. Since the wind blows   Dependent   Independent

5. The leaves fall to the ground   Dependent   Independent

6. While I rake the leaves   Dependent   Independent

7. The dog watches me closely   Dependent   Independent

8. As soon as I go inside   Dependent   Independent

9. The dog plays in the pile   Dependent   Independent

10. She has fun but makes a mess   Dependent   Independent

EXERCISE 5.4 — Independent and Dependent Clauses

Step 1: Double underline the <u>verbs</u> and underline the <u>subjects</u>.

Step 2: Look at the first word of the clause to see if it is a subordinating conjunction. If you find a subordinating conjunction, mark it with a <u>wavy underline</u>.

Step 3: If the clause has a subordinating conjunction, circle DEPENDENT. If it does not have a subordinating conjunction, circle INDEPENDENT.

EXAMPLE: The bamboo <u>lemur</u> <u>is</u> a rare species.   Dependent   (Independent)

1. Since it mostly eats bamboo   Dependent   Independent

2. It lives in bamboo forests   Dependent   Independent

3. Although its head and body are only sixteen inches long Dependent   Independent

4. Its tail is about twenty inches long   Dependent   Independent

5. Bamboo lemurs have soft fur and cute faces   Dependent   Independent

6. Because only 160 bamboo lemurs exist   Dependent   Independent

7. They are an endangered species   Dependent   Independent

8. The lemurs live on the island of Madagascar   Dependent   Independent

9. Where the forest shrinks each year   Dependent   Independent

10. Because farmers want more crop land   Dependent   Independent

Chapter 6

Sentence Types Part 2 — Simple, Compound, and Complex

You have already learned how to identify Simple and Compound sentences. Now that you know how to tell the difference between independent and dependent clauses, you can learn to identify Complex sentences.

EXERCISE 6.1 — Labeling Clauses

Some of these sentences have one clause and some of them have two clauses. Follow the steps to analyze each sentence:

Step 1:   Use the three time words (*yesterday, every day, tomorrow*) to find the verbs. Double underline the <u>verbs</u>.

Step 2:   Ask *"who or what did the verb?"* to find the subjects. Underline the <u>subjects</u>.

Step 3:   Look at the first word of each clause. If the first word is a subordinating conjunction, underline it with a <u>wavy underline</u>.

Step 4:   If a clause has a subordinating conjunction, label it **DC** for Dependent Clause. If it does not have a subordinating conjunction, label it **IC** for Independent Clause. You don't need to label any phrases.

EXAMPLE: Since <u>James</u> <u>got</u> some free tickets, <u>he</u> <u>went</u> to a Bulls baseball game.
            DC   IC

1.   The Durham Bulls played a great game; they won by seven runs.

2.   When their first batter hit a home run, the crowd cheered.

3.   The Bulls' pitcher stuck out most of the batters.

4.   When the other team made a hit, the Bulls' center fielder caught it.

5.   After the Bulls won the game, the coach congratulated all the players.

A SIMPLE SENTENCE has one independent clause.

> <u>Josephine</u> <u>wore</u> a purple velvet gown.
>   IC

A COMPOUND SENTENCE has two independent clauses.

> <u>Philip</u> <u>saw</u> Josephine; <u>he</u> <u>asked</u> her to dance.
>   IC   IC

A COMPLEX SENTENCE has one independent clause and one dependent clause.

> After <u>they</u> <u>danced</u>, <u>they</u> <u>drank</u> champagne.
>   DC   IC

> <u>They</u> <u>drank</u> champagne after <u>they</u> <u>danced</u>.
>   IC   DC

It doesn't matter whether the Dependent Clause comes first or last. As long as there is one of each, the sentence is complex.

Look carefully at the two complex sentences and see if you can find a tiny difference between them. The first sentence has a comma, and the second sentence doesn't. This is the correct way to write a complex sentence.

When the dependent clause comes first, put a comma between the two clauses, like this:

> Because only 160 bamboo <u>lemurs</u> <u>exist</u>, <u>they</u> <u>are</u> an endangered species
>   DC   IC

> Since <u>they</u> mostly <u>eat</u> bamboo, <u>lemurs</u> <u>live</u> in bamboo forests.
>   DC   IC

When the independent clause comes first, DON'T put a comma.

> <u>They</u> <u>are</u> an endangered species because only 160 bamboo <u>lemurs</u> <u>exist</u>.
>   IC   DC

> <u>Lemurs</u> <u>live</u> in bamboo forests since <u>they</u> mostly <u>eat</u> bamboo.
>   IC   DC

EXERCISE 6.2 — Complex Sentences with the Dependent Clause First

Follow the steps to analyze each sentence:

Step 1: Use the three time words (yesterday, every day, tomorrow) to find the verbs. Double underline the <u>verbs</u>.

Step 2: Ask "who or what did the verb?" to find the subjects. Underline the <u>subjects</u>.

Step 3: The first word of the sentence is a subordinating conjunction, so underline it with a <u>wavy underline</u>.

Step 4: Label the first clause DC for Dependent Clause, and label the second clause IC for for Independent Clause.

Step 5: Put a comma after the first clause (the dependent clause).

EXAMPLE: When <u>Karen</u> <u>bakes</u> apple pies, the <u>kitchen</u> <u>smells</u> great.
                    DC   IC

1. Since she puts in lots of sugar the green apples taste sweet.

2. Because her husband likes spicy pies she puts in plenty of cinnamon.

3. After she peels all the apples she puts the peels and cores into the compost bin.

4. When she rolls out the crust she sprinkles flour on the counter.

5. Although Karen is careful she usually spills some flour on the floor.

6. After she puts the pies in the oven she sweeps the floor.

7. Because she like the pies to be pretty Karen cuts a design in the top crust.

8. While the pies bake a delicious aroma fills the house.

9. When Karen serves the pie she puts a scoop of ice cream on each piece.

10. After her family eats pie their mouths are very happy.

Did you notice that the sentences were sounding all the same after a while? This is because they all have a dependent clause first and then an independent clause. Each sentence sounds fine by itself, but when you have ten sentences of the same kind in a row, it starts to sound boring. Beautiful and interesting writing has a mixture of different kinds of sentences.

EXERCISE 6.3 — Mixed Complex Sentences

Follow the steps to analyze each sentence:

Step 1: Use the three time words (yesterday, every day, tomorrow) to find the verbs. Double underline the verbs.

Step 2: Ask "who or what did the verb?" to find the subjects. Underline the subjects.

Step 3: Look at the first word of each clause. If the first word is a subordinating conjunction, underline it with a wavy underline.

Step 4: If a clause has a subordinating conjunction, label it DC for Dependent Clause. If it does not have a subordinating conjunction, label it IC for Independent Clause.

Step 5: If the DC comes first, put a comma after it. If the IC comes first, don't put a comma.

EXAMPLE: Farmers in India are relieved when the monsoon arrives.
                       IC   DC

1. Before the rainy season begins the weather is very hot and dry.

2. Farmers can't water their crops because their wells are dry.

3. Although trucks bring water to the villages people have to save that water for drinking.

4. Some families visit temples because they want to pray for rain.

5. People know that climate change is responsible for the dry weather.

6. Many people feel better after they pray.

7. Although monsoon was always hard to predict global warming has made things worse.

8. Some villages dug canals because they wanted to save every drop of rain.

9. When the monsoon finally comes the rain falls hard for four months.

10. After the rain ends farmers live through seven months of drought once again.

EXERCISE 6.4 — Mixed Complex Sentences

Follow the steps to analyze each sentence:

Step 1: Use the three time words (yesterday, every day, tomorrow) to find the verbs. Double underline the verbs.

Step 2: Ask "who or what did the verb?" to find the subjects. Underline the subjects.

Step 3: Look at the first word of each clause. If the first word is a subordinating conjunction, underline it with a wavy underline.

Step 4: If a clause has a subordinating conjunction, label it DC for Dependent Clause. If it does not have a subordinating conjunction, label it IC for Independent Clause.

Step 5: If the DC comes first, put a comma after it. If the IC comes first, don't put a comma.

EXAMPLE: When the Fourth of July arrives, Mike sets up his grill.
            DC   IC

1. Mike grills hot dogs since his kids love them.

2. While the hot dogs are cooking the kids make ice cream.

3. Although the kids take turns at the crank their arms get tired.

4. Turning the crank gets harder as the ice cream freezes.

5. When dinner is ready everyone is starving.

6. The kids enjoy eating watermelon because they like to spit the seeds.

7. After they finish eating Mike drives the kids to the park to see the fireworks.

8. Mike leaves the dog at home because the dog is afraid of firecrackers.

9. When the sky turns dark the fireworks begin.

10. While the people enjoy the show the mosquitoes have their own meal.

EXERCISE 6.5 — Simple and Complex Sentences

Follow the steps to analyze each sentence:

Step 1: Use the three time words (*yesterday, every day, tomorrow*) to find the verbs. Double underline the verbs.

Step 2: Ask *"who or what did the verb?"* to find the subjects. Underline the subjects.

Step 3: Look at the first word of each clause. If the first word is a subordinating conjunction, underline it with a wavy underline.

Step 4: If a clause has a subordinating conjunction, label it **DC** for Dependent Clause. If it does not have a subordinating conjunction, label it **IC** for Independent Clause.

Step 5: If the sentence has one independent clause, circle **S** for Simple. If it has an independent clause and a dependent clause, circle **CX** for Complex.

EXAMPLE: While she is at the fair, Jamie plays carnival games.   S   (CX)
           DC   IC

1. Jamie loves the ring toss.   S   CX

2. When she looks at the prizes, she wants to win one.   S   CX

3. Although Jamie usually loses, she keeps playing.   S   CX

4. Jamie spent a lot of money on the ring toss game.   S   CX

5. Since she kept trying, Jamie finally won a stuffed animal.   S   CX

EXERCISE 6.6 — Complex and Compound Sentences

Follow the steps to analyze each sentence:

Step 1: Use the three time words (*yesterday, every day, tomorrow*) to find the verbs. Double underline the <u>verbs</u>.

Step 2: Ask *"who or what did the verb?"* to find the subjects. Underline the <u>subjects</u>.

Step 3: Look at the first word of each clause. If the first word is a subordinating conjunction, underline it with a <u>wavy underline</u>.

Step 4: If a clause has a subordinating conjunction, label it **DC** for Dependent Clause. If it does not have a subordinating conjunction, label it **IC** for Independent Clause.

Step 5: If the sentence has two independent clauses, label it **CP** for Compound. If the sentence has one independent clause and one dependent clause, label it **CX** for Complex.

EXAMPLE: When Jamie goes to the fair, she always rides the roller coaster.   CP   (CX)
                   DC   IC

1. Jamie went to the ticket booth; she bought twenty ride tickets.   CP   CX

2. She looked at the roller coaster; it had a really long line.   CP   CX

3. She went on the tilt-a-whirl because it had a short line.   CP   CX

4. After she rode the tilt-a-whirl, Jamie rode the Zipper.   CP   CX

5. The roller coaster still had a long line; Jamie went in the fun house.   CP   CX

6. She stood in line at the roller coaster because she only had four tickets left.   CP   CX

7. Since it was a hot day, Jamie was sweaty and thirsty.   CP   CX

8. If she bought a drink, she would lose her place in line.   CP   CX

9. She decided to wait; it was her turn at last!   CP   CX

10. The roller coaster ride was great; it was worth the wait.   CP   CX

EXERCISE 6.7 — Complex and Compound Sentences

Follow the steps to analyze each sentence:

Step 1: Use the three time words (*yesterday, every day, tomorrow*) to find the verbs. Double underline the <u>verbs</u>.

Step 2: Ask *"who or what did the verb?"* to find the subjects. Underline the <u>subjects</u>.

Step 3: Look at the first word of each clause. If the first word is a subordinating conjunction, underline it with a wavy underline.

Step 4: If a clause has a subordinating conjunction, label it **DC** for Dependent Clause. If it does not have a subordinating conjunction, label it **IC** for Independent Clause.

Step 5: If the sentence has two independent clauses, label it **CP** for Compound. If the sentence has one independent clause and one dependent clause, label it **CX** for Complex.

EXAMPLE: <u>Americans</u> <u>love</u> ice cream; <u>we</u> <u>eat</u> an average of six gallons per year.   (CP)   CX
                    IC   IC

1. Although vanilla is the most popular flavor, chocolate comes in second.   CP   CX

2. Ice cream sundaes are delicious, and they have an interesting history.   CP   CX

3. When soda was first invented, it was mixed like a cocktail.   CP   CX

4. The customer chose a flavor, and the waiter blended the syrup with soda water. CP   CX

5. Soda was a popular drink six days a week, but it was banned on Sundays.   CP   CX

6. Since soda was considered improper, stores couldn't sell it on Sundays.   CP   CX

7. A clever store owner solved the problem when he invented a new treat.   CP   CX

8. He mixed the syrup with ice cream, and he served it in a bowl.   CP   CX

9. He called the creation a sundae because it could be eaten on Sundays.   CP   CX

10. Modern Americans eat lots of ice cream, and we drink soda every day.   CP   CX

EXERCISE 6.8 — Simple, Compound, and Complex Sentences

Follow the steps to analyze each sentence:

Step 1:   Double underline the verbs.

Step 2:   Underline the subjects.

Step 3:   Mark any subordinating conjunctions with a wavy underline.

Step 4:   Label each clause with **DC** for Dependent Clause or **IC** for Independent Clause.

Step 5:   Circle **S** for Simple, **CP** for Compound, or **CX** for Complex.

EXAMPLE: Caroline has two gerbils; their names are Caramel and Mole.   S   (CP)   CX
                    IC   IC

1. Caramel is light brown, and Mole is gray and white.   S   CP   CX

2. The gerbils love to chew things.   S   CP   CX

3. When Caroline puts a twig in their cage, it is gone by the next day.   S   CP   CX

4. The gerbils run around the room, and they hide under the furniture.   S   CP   CX

5. They are hard to catch because they are fast and slippery.   S   CP   CX

6. Caramel is bold, but Mole is nervous and timid.   S   CP   CX

7. Caramel will climb up onto Caroline's lap.   S   CP   CX

8. When Caroline catches Mole, he tries to run away.   S   CP   CX

9. Both gerbils are really cute.   S   CP   CX

10. Carmel and Mole are great pets, and they never make noise.   S   CP   CX

EXERCISE 6.9 — Simple, Compound, and Complex Sentences

Follow the steps to analyze each sentence:

Step 1:   Double underline the <u>verbs</u>.

Step 2:   Underline the <u>subjects</u>.

Step 3:   Mark any subordinating conjunctions with a <u>wavy underline</u>.

Step 4:   Label each clause with **DC** for Dependent Clause or **IC** for Independent Clause.

Step 5:   Circle **S** for Simple, **CP** for Compound, or **CX** for Complex.

EXAMPLE: The planet <u>Zigland</u> <u>exists</u> in a galaxy far, far away.   (S)   CP   CX
                                        IC

1. Zork and Zink were scientists from the planet Zigland.   S   CP   CX

2. They traveled a million miles; they wanted to visit Earth.   S   CP   CX

3. When they landed on Earth, they were surprised.   S   CP   CX

4. On Zigland the grass was purple, and the sky was yellow.   S   CP   CX

5. After they climbed down from their space ship, Zork and Zink went exploring.   S   CP   CX

6. They gathered plant specimens and water samples.   S   CP   CX

7. They interviewed Earth animals, but they couldn't communicate very well.   S   CP   CX

8. Since Zork and Zink were the size of mice, the cat tried to eat them!   S   CP   CX

9. The tiny scientists raced back to their ship.   S   CP   CX

10. After they survived this near-death experience, they returned to Zigland as heroes. S   CP   CX

EXERCISE 6.10 — Simple, Compound, and Complex Sentences

Follow the steps to analyze each sentence:

Step 1:   Double underline the <u>verbs</u>.

Step 2:   Underline the <u>subjects</u>.

Step 3:   Mark any subordinating conjunctions with a <u>wavy underline</u>.

Step 4:   Label each clause with **DC** for Dependent Clause or **IC** for Independent Clause.

Step 5:   Circle **S** for Simple, **CP** for Compound, or **CX** for Complex.

EXAMPLE: <u>The Statue of Liberty</u> <u>is</u> a famous landmark in New York City.   Ⓢ CP CX
           IC

1. The statue holds a torch in her right hand; her left hand holds a tablet.   S   CP CX

2. Since the U.S. declared independence on July 4, 1776, this date is inscribed

    on the tablet.   S   CP CX

3. The statue was a gift to America from the people of France.   S   CP CX

4. Her crown has seven spokes; these represent the seven seas and the

    seven continents.   S   CP CX

5. A broken chain at her feet represents breaking free from tyranny.   S   CP CX

6. After the French sculptor finished the statue, he took it apart for shipping.   S   CP CX

7. The sculptor spent several years putting the statue back together in the U.S.   S   CP CX

8. The statue is hollow, and it has stairs leading up to the crown.   S   CP CX

9. Visitors can climb to the top if they are physically fit.   S   CP CX

10. The statue was completed in 1884; it is still a symbol of freedom.   S   CP CX

Chapter 7

Sentence Fragments

A correct sentence must have at least one independent clause. **A FRAGMENT is a sentence that doesn't have an independent clause.**

REMEMBER:

A PHRASE is a group of words that does not have a subject and a verb. Maybe it has a verb but no subject, or maybe it has a subject but no verb, or maybe it doesn't have either one. One kind of phrase is a prepositional phrase, but there are many other kinds of phrases too.

> in the morning

> going to the movies

A CLAUSE is a group of words that has a subject and a verb. An INDEPENDENT clause is a clause that can stand alone because it sounds finished and it expresses a complete idea.

> Jamie hit the winning run.

> The weather was cold.

A DEPENDENT clause is a clause that can not stand alone because it leaves the reader asking "What happened?" A dependent clause starts with a SUBORDINATING CONJUNCTION that changes the sound of the clause.

> After Jamie hit the winning run . . .   what happened?

> Although the weather was cold . . .   what?

Common Subordinating Conjunctions				
after	although	as	because	before
if	since	so that	that	though
till/until	unless	when	where	while

45

A FRAGMENT is a sentence that does not have an independent clause. It has only a dependent clause or a phrase. Dependent clauses and phrases are useful parts of a sentence. They can add details and make a sentence more interesting. But they can not be sentences by themselves. A correct sentence must have at least one independent clause.

Fragments are common mistakes that lots of people make when they write. But fragments make your writing hard to understand.

After Jamie hit the winning run.   Fragment!

Going to the movies.   Fragment!

Learning to find and fix the fragments in your own writing will make a big difference in your grades in college and also in how well people can understand what you write.

EXERCISE 7.1 — Finding Fragments

First <u>double underline</u> the verbs and <u>underline</u> the subjects. If a sentence is missing a verb or a subject, it is a phrase. Circle **Fragment**.

If a sentence has a subject and a verb, it is a clause. Now look for a subordinating conjunction. This would be the first word of the sentence. If you find a subordinating conjunction, mark it with a <u>wavy underline</u>. The sentence is a dependent clause. Circle **Fragment**.

If a sentence has a subject and a verb and it does **not** have a subordinating conjunction, it is an independent clause. Circle **Correct.**

EXAMPLE:	Since his daughter loves swinging.	Correct	(Fragment)
1.	Shawn built a swing set.	Correct	Fragment
2.	Went to the lumber yard.	Correct	Fragment
3.	So that he could buy the wood.	Correct	Fragment
4.	Bought a new blade for his saw.	Correct	Fragment
5.	Shawn started cutting the wood.	Correct	Fragment
6.	A very loud noise and a mess of saw dust.	Correct	Fragment
7.	After he finished cutting the wood.	Correct	Fragment
8.	Shawn drilled the holes.	Correct	Fragment
9.	Bolted the pieces together.	Correct	Fragment
10.	He finished it with a coat of stain.	Correct	Fragment

EXERCISE 7.2 — Finding Fragments

First <u>double underline</u> the verbs and <u>underline</u> the subjects. If a sentence is missing a verb or a subject, it is a phrase. Circle **Fragment**.

If a sentence has a subject and a verb, it is a clause. Now look for a subordinating conjunction. This would be the first word of the sentence. If you find a subordinating conjunction, mark it with a <u>wavy underline</u>. The sentence is a dependent clause. Circle **Fragment**.

If a sentence has a subject and a verb and it does **not** have a subordinating conjunction, it is an independent clause. Circle **Correct**.

EXAMPLE: Because a cat has no collarbone.	Correct	(Fragment)
1. A cat will squeeze through a hole.	Correct	Fragment
2. No larger than its head.	Correct	Fragment
3. Cats purr twenty-six times per second.	Correct	Fragment
4. The same speed as an idling diesel truck.	Correct	Fragment
5. If the cat's name ends with an EE sound.	Correct	Fragment
6. Like Kitty or Molly or Sammy.	Correct	Fragment
7. The cat will respond to its name more quickly.	Correct	Fragment
8. A cat will jump.	Correct	Fragment
9. Five times as high as the length of its tail.	Correct	Fragment
10. Domestic cats sprint thirty miles per hour.	Correct	Fragment

EXERCISE 7.3 — Finding Fragments

First <u>double underline</u> the verbs and <u>underline</u> the subjects. If a sentence is missing a verb or a subject, it is a phrase. Circle **Fragment.**

If a sentence has a subject and a verb, it is a clause. Now look for a subordinating conjunction. This would be the first word of the sentence. If you find a subordinating conjunction, mark it with a <u>wavy underline</u>. The sentence is a dependent clause. Circle **Fragment.**

If a sentence has a subject and a verb and it does **not** have a subordinating conjunction, it is an independent clause. Circle **Correct.**

	EXAMPLE: Denim <u>fabric</u> <u>was</u> invented.	(Correct)	Fragment
1.	In the sixteenth century.	Correct	Fragment
2.	The French called the fabric "genes."	Correct	Fragment
3.	Because it came from the town of Genoa in Italy.	Correct	Fragment
4.	Denim pants were called jeans.	Correct	Fragment
5.	The cloth was made from cotton.	Correct	Fragment
6.	People liked denim.	Correct	Fragment
7.	Because it remained durable.	Correct	Fragment
8.	Even after many washings.	Correct	Fragment
9.	Factories produce lots of denim fabric.	Correct	Fragment
10.	About 2.5 billion yards per year.	Correct	Fragment

Fixing Fragments

There are two ways to fix a fragment. We will learn them one at a time.

FIRST METHOD: Erase a period and attach the fragment to another sentence. This method works for both kinds of fragments — phrases and dependent clauses.

> Sharon <u>felt</u> sleepy. During her afternoon class.
> Correct sentence   Fragment
>
> Sharon <u>felt</u> sleepy during her afternoon class.
> Correct sentence

EXERCISE 7.4 — Fixing Fragments by Erasing a Period

Mark the <u>verbs</u>, <u>subjects</u>, and any <u>subordinating conjunctions</u>. Cross out a period and make the capital letter lower case to join the fragment and the independent clause into one long sentence.

   EXAMPLE: Between her classes, <u>Sharon</u> <u>got</u> a latte.

1.   She really needed the caffeine. To wake herself up.

2.   Because she stopped to buy a latte. Sharon was late to class.

3.   The teacher gave Sharon a dirty look. When she came in late.

4.   Sharon sipped her latte. While the teacher droned on about reducing fractions.

5.   When class ended. Sharon was wide awake and feeling great.

SECOND METHOD: If the fragment is a dependent clause, you can fix it by erasing the subordinating conjunction. When you erase the subordinating conjunction, you change the clause from dependent to independent.

When the dog chews the newspaper.	Dependent clause — Fragment!
The dog chews the newspaper.	Independent clause — Correct!
After Sally bought a new car.	Dependent clause — Fragment!
Sally bought a new car.	Independent clause — Correct!

EXERCISE 7.5 — Fixing Fragments by Erasing a Subordinating Conjunction

Mark the verbs, subjects, and subordinating conjunctions. Cross out the subordinating conjunction to turn the dependent clause (fragment) into an independent clause (correct sentence).

EXAMPLE: When Steve plays football.

1.   After Isaac mowed the lawn.

2.   Since it was my birthday.

3.   Because Alexa overslept and missed class.

4.   If Jason won the race.

5.   While we watched the movie.

EXERCISE 7.6 — Finding and Fixing Fragments

Mark the <u>verbs</u>, <u>subjects</u>, and <u>subordinating conjunctions</u>. Under each sentence, write OK if it is a correct sentence and FRAG if it is a fragment. Fix each fragment by crossing out a period or by crossing out a subordinating conjunction.

Gloria has a big black cat. Named Inky. Inky gets into trouble. For clawing the furniture. Although

Gloria bought him a scratching post. Inky prefers to claw the couch. When he goes outside. He tries

to catch birds. Inky will stalk a bird through the grass. Pretending to be a panther stalking an antelope.

Inky will eat the head. Off the bird. And leave the body on the door step. He wants to show off his

hunting abilities.

EXERCISE 7.7 — Finding and Fixing Fragments

Mark the <u>verbs</u>, <u>subjects</u>, and <u>subordinating conjunctions</u>. Under each sentence, write OK if it is a correct sentence and FRAG if it is a fragment. Fix each fragment by crossing out a period or by crossing out a subordinating conjunction.

The seahorse is a remarkable creature. Although it looks like a tiny horse. It is a fish. Seahorses mate

for life. Each morning the married couple dances together. To reaffirm their commitment to each other.

If one seahorse dies. The other seahorse waits a long time before finding a new mate. Since seahorses

move slowly. They rely on camouflage for protection. They quickly change color. To blend in with their

surroundings. Seahorses are a popular food in Asia. China consumes over six millions seahorses a year.

For food, medicine, and even aphrodisiacs.

EXERCISE 7.8 — Finding and Fixing Fragments

Mark the <u>verbs</u>, <u>subjects</u>, and subordinating conjunctions. Under each sentence, write OK if it is a correct sentence and FRAG if it is a fragment. Fix each fragment by crossing out a period or by crossing out a subordinating conjunction.

If you eat ice cream too quickly. You will get a brain freeze. The pain is caused by cold food or

drink hitting the roof of your mouth. Because the cold causes the blood vessels to constrict. The pain

peaks about forty seconds. After you eat or drink something too cold. The freeze passes in about ninety

seconds. Although brain freeze can happen anytime. It is most common on a very hot day. When you

are overheated. To avoid a brain freeze. You can eat the ice cream more slowly.

Chapter 8

Finding Comma Splices and Run-ons

As you know, every sentence must have an independent clause. A sentence that doesn't have an independent clause is a **fragment.**

Can a sentence have two independent clauses? Yes, it can. When you write a sentence with two independent clauses, you must be careful about how you join the two clauses together. If you're not careful, you could accidently write a comma splice or a run-on sentence.

Both a comma splice and a run-on sentence have two independent clauses, and the independent clauses are not joined correctly.

      Sue <u>cooked</u> dinner, <u>Joe</u> <u>washed</u> the dishes.   Comma splice

      Sue <u>cooked</u> dinner <u>Joe</u> <u>washed</u> the dishes.   Run-on sentence

Look carefully at these two sentences and see what the difference is between them; it's a very tiny difference. **The comma splice has a comma and the run-on does not have a comma.** That's the only difference. Both sentences have two independent clauses.

      Sue <u>cooked</u> dinner <u>Joe</u> <u>washed</u> the dishes.
         IC   IC

EXERCISE 8.1 — Comma Splices and Run-ons

Mark the <u>verbs</u> and the <u>subjects.</u> Look and see if a comma comes between the two clauses. If you find a comma, circle **CS** for comma splice. If you don't find a comma, circle **RO** for run-on.

EXAMPLE: <u>Benjamin Franklin</u> <u>was</u> a great man <u>he</u> <u>lived</u> in Philadelphia.   CS   (RO)

1. Ben was born in 1706, he had sixteen brothers and sisters!   CS   RO

2. Ben wanted to be a writer he worked in his brother's printing shop.   CS   RO

3. Ben was born in Boston he moved to Philadelphia.   CS   RO

4. Ben fell in love with Deborah, they got married.   CS   RO

5. Ben started a newspaper it was called *The Pennsylvania Gazette.*   CS   RO

6. Ben was successful, he became famous.   CS   RO

7. Ben was also an inventor, he invented the wood stove.   CS   RO

8. Lightning causes many fires he invented the lightning rod.   CS   RO

9. Ben traveled to England, he encouraged the king to be nice to America.   CS   RO

10. Ben signed the Declaration of Independence he signed the Constitution.   CS   RO

EXERCISE 8.2 — Comma Splices and Run-ons

Mark the <u>verbs</u> and the <u>subjects.</u> Look and see if a comma comes between the two clauses. If you find a comma, circle **CS** for comma splice. If you don't find a comma, circle **RO** for run-on.

EXAMPLE: The first <u>cookies</u> <u>were</u> baked in Persia <u>Persia</u> <u>is</u> present-day Iran.   CS   (RO)

1. Persians began baking cookies in the seventeenth century, Persia was one

    of the first countries to make sugar.   CS   RO

2. The Dutch call cookies "koekje" (kook-yah), this means little cake.   CS   RO

3. Germans use the term "keks" Italians call them "biscotti."   CS   RO

4. Americans love cookies, our favorite is chocolate chip.   CS   RO

5. Chocolate chip cookies were invented in 1930, they were created by accident.   CS   RO

6. Ruth Wakefield was baking cookies at the Toll House Inn she ran out of

    baker's chocolate.   CS   RO

7. She had a friend named Andrew Nestle, he gave her some bars of

    semi-sweet chocolate.   CS   RO

8. Ruth broke the chocolate bars into little pieces she mixed the pieces into

    her cookie dough.   CS   RO

9. Ruth expected the chocolate to melt the chocolate stayed in chunks.   CS   RO

10. She made the first chocolate chip cookies, everyone loved her accident.   CS   RO

Fixing Comma Splices and Run-ons

When you write a sentence with two independent clauses, there are three ways that you can join the clauses correctly and avoid writing a comma splice or run-on sentence. We will learn them one at a time.

First Method — Semi-colon

A semi-colon looks like exactly what it is: a period mixed with a comma. A semi-colon is halfway between a period and a comma. A period would separate the two clauses into two separate sentences. A comma is too small to separate independent clauses. So a semi-colon is big enough to separate them, but small enough that they are still one sentence.

> <u>Sue</u> <u>cooked</u> dinner; <u>Joe</u> <u>washed</u> the dishes.

EXERCISE 8.3 — Sentences with Semi-Colons

Mark the <u>verbs</u> and the <u>subjects</u>. Put a semi-colon in the spot where the two independent clauses come together.

> EXAMPLE: A <u>frog</u> <u>lived</u> in the pond; <u>he</u> <u>was</u> green.

1.   The frog had strong legs he was a good swimmer.

2.   His tongue was sticky he caught bugs with it.

3.   He loved flies flies were delicious like candy.

4.   Mosquitos were sour he did not like them.

5.   At night the frog sat on his rock he ribbited loudly to the moon.

Second Method — Comma with a Coordinating Conjunction

The second way to join two independent clauses is to **put a comma and a coordinating conjunction between the clauses.**

Sue <u>cooked</u> dinner, and <u>Joe</u> <u>washed</u> the dishes.

for
and
nor
but
or
yet
so

There are only seven **coordinating conjunctions**, and they are very special words. They are all little–only two or three letters long–but they are very useful in grammar. The words can be arranged so that their first letters spell **FANBOYS.**

When we first learned about **subordinating conjunctions**, we looked at some words that begin with the prefix SUB: submarine, subway, submissive. We saw how the prefix SUB means below or less. That is what a subordinating conjunction does. It makes a clause dependent, unable to stand alone, because the clause sound unfinished.

After <u>we</u> <u>watched</u> the movie. . . .   WHAT HAPPENED?

Now think of some words that begin with the prefix CO: cooperate, coworker, coexist. **The prefix CO means together or equal.** When you cooperate, you work with someone as equals. Your coworker is not your boss or your employee; you are equals. Animals that coexist live side-by-side with each other. This is a very different meaning than SUB.

A coordinating conjunction joins things that are equal, such as two independent clauses.

How can you tell the difference between a coordinating conjunction and a subordinating conjunction? Since there are only seven coordinating conjunctions, it is not too hard just to remember them with FANBOYS. Also, you can just look at the lists of coordinating and subordinating conjunctions.

Common Subordinating Conjunctions				
after	although	as	because	before
if	since	so that	that	though
till/until	unless	when	where	while

EXERCISE 8.4 — Identifying Subordinating and Coordinating Conjunctions

Write each of the following words on the correct side: because, after, and, since, while, for, when, so, if, nor, but, so that, although, or, until

Subordinating	Coordinating

EXERCISE 8.5 — Sentences with Coordinating Conjunctions

Mark the <u>verbs</u> and the <u>subjects</u>. Find the coordinating conjunction that comes between the two independent clauses. **Put a comma in front of the coordinating conjunction.**

  EXAMPLE: <u>Mike</u> <u>is</u> allergic to fur, so <u>he</u> <u>has</u> a pet lizard.

1.   The lizard has smooth skin but Mike named him Fuzzy.

2.   Fuzzy is green and he has beady black eyes.

3.   He is four inches long but he will grow to be one foot long.

4.   Fuzzy is very quiet so Mike's neighbors never complain about barking.

5.   Mike will buy another lizard or he will get a pet snake.

EXERCISE 8.6 — Fixing Comma Splices and Run-ons with a Coordinating Conjunction or a Semi-colon

Mark the <u>verbs</u> and the <u>subjects</u>. Find the spot where the two independent clauses come together. Add a comma and whichever coordinating conjunction sounds good, OR add a semi-colon.

EXAMPLE: Tropical <u>storms</u> <u>occur</u> every year; <u>they</u> <u>are</u> dangerous and inconvenient.

1.   Tropical storms in the Atlantic are called hurricanes tropical storms in the Pacific or Indian Ocean are called typhoons.

2.   Hurricanes have strong winds they bring lots of rain.

3.   The wind and rain damage property they endanger people and animals.

4.   Fortunately, meteorologists predict hurricanes people have time to prepare.

5.   Meteorologists give general information about a hurricane no one knows the exactly what to expect.

6.   A family can stay at home during a hurricane they can evacuate.

7.   The storm passes in one day the electricity is out for a week.

8.   Meals of canned food become boring cooking over sterno is a challenge.

9.   The shower is freezing cold the water heater doesn't work without electricity.

10. People rejoice at the return of electricity life can get back to normal.

EXERCISE 8.7 — Fixing Comma Splices and Run-ons with a Coordinating Conjunction or a Semi-colon

Mark the <u>verbs</u> and the <u>subjects</u>. Find the spot where the two independent clauses come together. Add a comma and whichever coordinating conjunction sounds good, OR add a semi-colon.

EXAMPLE: <u>Roller coasters</u> <u>are</u> popular today, but <u>they</u> <u>were</u> invented in the 1700s.

1.   Russians carved steep slides out of ice people slid down like on a water slide.

2.   A French businessman liked the Russian slide he built one in France.

3.   The weather in France was too warm his ice slide turned to slush.

4.   He built a slide out of waxed wood he made little carts with rollers on their bottoms.

5.   This slide was dangerous many people had accidents.

6.   The Frenchman added a track to his slide he wanted people to keep riding it.

7.   The track made the slide safer the new roller coaster was a big hit.

8.   In America, coal mines used train tracks for moving carts of coal the miners enjoyed zooming down the steep track in the empty carts.

9.   In 1870, one coal mine opened its track to the public people paid one dollar for a ride.

10. The ride reached one hundred miles per hour this first roller coaster never had any accidents.

EXERCISE 8.8 — Fixing Comma Splices and Run-ons with a Coordinating Conjunction or a Semi-colon

Mark the <u>verbs</u> and the <u>subjects</u>. Find the spot where the two independent clauses come together. Add a comma and whichever coordinating conjunction sounds good, OR add a semi-colon.

EXAMPLE: Some <u>butterflies</u> <u>live</u> for only a few weeks, but <u>others</u> <u>hibernate</u> through the winter.

1. Hibernating butterflies need protection from wind they cling to sheltered tree branches.

2. The spring sun warms the butterfly it wakes up and begins to move.

3. The butterfly flies away it finds a mate.

4. Birds eat some butterflies other butterflies taste bad.

5. Native Americans value butterflies they ask butterflies to carry a wish to the Great Spirit.

6. Some nursing homes have butterfly rooms Alzheimer's patients enjoy watching the butterflies.

7. The patients wait for the butterfly to hatch from the cocoon they watch the butterflies grow.

8. In Appalachia brides hope to see a butterfly on their wedding day a butterfly is a sign of good luck in marriage.

9. Some brides want lots of butterflies they purchase butterflies for their wedding.

10. At the end of the wedding, the guests receive envelopes of butterflies they open the envelopes to release a cloud of beauty.

Third Method — Subordinating Conjunction

The last method is sneaky. You can add a subordinating conjunction and turn one of the clauses into a dependent clause. Since a comma splice or run-on has two independent clauses, if you turn one of the independent clauses into a dependent clause, you've fixed the CS or RO.

You can add a subordinating conjunction to the first clause or to the second clause.

> After Sue cooked dinner, Joe washed the dishes.
>   DC   IC

> Joe washed the dishes after Sue cooked dinner.
>   IC   DC

Look carefully at these two sentences, and you will see a tiny difference. The first sentence, where the dependent clause comes first, has a comma after the dependent clause. The second sentence, where the independent clause comes first, does not have a comma.

Use whichever subordinating conjunction suits the meaning of your sentence. Remember to add only one subordinating conjunction though. If you make both clauses dependent, you'll have a fragment.

> After Sue cooked dinner, before Joe washed the dishes . . .   what happened?   **Fragment!**

Common Subordinating Conjunctions				
after	although	as	because	before
if	since	so that	that	though
till/until	unless	when	where	while

EXERCISE 8.9 — Fixing Comma Splices and Run-ons with a Subordinating Conjunction

Mark the <u>verbs</u> and the <u>subjects</u>. Then fix the comma splice or run-on by adding a subordinating conjunction in the empty space to make one of the clauses dependent. Use whichever subordinating conjunction you think will sound best. If you make the first clause dependent, put a comma after it. If you make the second clause dependent, you don't need to add a comma.

EXAMPLE: Although   <u>Dinosaurs</u> <u>lived</u> long ago, <u>they</u> <u>are</u> extinct now.

1. "Dinosaur" means terrible lizard _____ dinosaurs were huge reptiles.

2. _____ some dinosaurs ate meat others ate plants.

3. Most mother dinosaurs abandoned their nests _____ they laid their eggs.

4. _____ some big dinosaurs ate little ones the little ones were fast runners.

5. Scientists dig up dinosaur bones _____ they can study the fossils.

Common Subordinating Conjunctions				
after	although	as	because	before
if	since	so that	that	though
till/until	unless	when	where	while

EXERCISE 8.10 — Fixing Comma Splices and Run-ons with a Subordinating Conjunction

Mark the <u>verbs</u> and the <u>subjects</u>. Then fix the comma splice or run-on by adding a subordinating conjunction to make one of the clauses dependent. Use whichever subordinating conjunction you think will sound best. If you make the first clause dependent, put a comma after it. If you make the second clause dependent, you don't need to add a comma.

EXAMPLE: <u>Frogs</u> <u>are</u> called amphibians because <u>amphibian</u> <u>means</u> double life.

1. _____ frogs lay eggs the eggs hatch in the water.

2. Frog babies are tadpoles _____ they look like little fish.

3. Tadpoles breathe with gills _____ they do not have lungs yet.

4. _____ tadpoles go through metamorphosis their bodies change.

5. Their tails get smaller _____ their arms and legs start to grow.

6. _____ they breathe with gills they also breathe some air.

7. _____ a tadpole is a little frog it hops out of the water.

8. The little frog grows _____ it becomes a big frog.

9. _____ the frog eats bugs it has a sticky tongue.

10. I like frogs _____ they eat mosquitoes.

Common Subordinating Conjunctions				
after	although	as	because	before
if	since	so that	that	though
till/until	unless	when	where	while

EXERCISE 8.11 — Fixing Comma Splices and Run-ons with Any Method You Like

Mark the <u>verbs</u> and the <u>subjects</u>. Then re-write the sentence to fix the comma splice or run-on using whichever method you think will sound best for that sentence.

      Method 1: add a semi-colon

      Method 2: add a comma and a coordinating conjunction

      Method 3: add a subordinating conjunction

    EXAMPLE: <u>Napoleon</u> <u>was</u> born in 1769, and <u>he</u> <u>died</u> in 1821.

1. The government was weak Napoleon became the leader of France.

2. In paintings Napoleon has his hand inside his vest this was a common pose in France.

3. Napoleon was not short he was the average height for men at that time.

4. People thought of Napoleon as short his friends were very tall.

5. Napoleon fought many wars over five million people died.

6. Napoleon was not all bad he did some good things.

7. France had 14,000 confusing laws Napoleon made them into seven simple laws.

8. His army conquered Spain Napoleon stopped the Inquisition.

9. The Inquisition killed non-Christians it burned them at the stake.

10. Napoleon ended the Inquisition he saved many people's lives.

EXERCISE 8.12 — Fixing Comma Splices and Run-ons with Any Method You Like

Mark the <u>verbs</u> and the <u>subjects</u>. Then re-write the sentence to fix the comma splice or run-on using whichever method you think will sound best for that sentence.

Method 1: add a semi-colon

Method 2: add a comma and a coordinating conjunction

Method 3: add a subordinating conjunction

EXAMPLE: <u>Baseball</u> <u>is</u> the all-American sport; <u>it</u> <u>has</u> a long history.

1. Abner Doubleday was a West Point cadet he invented modern baseball in 1839.

2. Abner lived in Cooperstown, New York, the Baseball Hall of Fame was built in Cooperstown.

3. Abner improved the game of baseball he didn't invent it by himself.

4. A similar game is much older it was played in 1744.

5. Early baseball was different in several ways it had only two bases.

6. Today bases are bags in 1744 the bases were posts.

7. The runner ran around the bases he did not touch the posts.

8. The pitcher threw underhanded the bat was flat and wide.

9. In 1778 American soldiers lived at Valley Forge they played a type of baseball.

10. In 1820 baseball was a popular sport at Harvard many students played for fun.

Chapter 9

Capitals and Quotations

Capital Letters

Use a capital letter at the beginning of a sentence. Use a capital letter for I. Use a capital letter for people's names.

Sharon asked Sarah, Melissa, and Tiffany to be her bridesmaids.

Mr. Smith invited Mrs. Smith, Rev. Jones, and Miss Baxter to play golf.

After dinner, I ate dessert, and then I cleared the table.

EXERCISE 9.1 — Capital Letters

Correct the capitalization in these sentences.

EXAMPLE: Sharon is getting married next month.

1. her fiancé's name is thomas.

2. sharon's bridesmaids will be her sisters sarah, melissa, and tiffany.

3. the ushers will be joe, brian, and jake.

4. i am helping sharon plan her wedding.

5. reverend jackson will perform the ceremony.

More Capitals

Capitalize family titles when you could replace the title with the person's name.

> When Mom and Dad got home, Grandma said the kids had been very good.

Mom, Dad, and Grandma are capitalized because those titles could be replaced with the people's names and the sentence would still sound right:

> When Mary and Steve got home, Barbara said the kids had been very good.

Now look at this sentence:

> My mom gave my dad a sweater for his birthday.

How would it sound if the titles were replaced with the names?

> My Mary gave my Steve a sweater for his birthday.

That sounds funny. If you can't replace the title (mom) with the person's name (Mary), don't use a capital.

Also use a capital for names of the days of the week, the months of the year, and holidays:

> This year Christmas is on a Monday.

> This year Easter is on April 16.

EXERCISE 9.2 — More Capitals

Correct the capitalization in these sentences.

EXAMPLE: This year Christmas is on a Monday.

1. we will go to my grandma's house for dinner.

2. grandma makes great christmas cookies.

3. mom always bakes pumpkin pie for thanksgiving.

4. thanksgiving is at the end of november.

5. my dad loves thanksgiving because he likes to eat.

6. after dinner dad washes the dishes so mom can rest.

7. dad knows that mom is tired after cooking all day.

8. my grandpa's favorite holiday is easter.

9. chocolate bunnies are grandpa's favorite treat.

10. on saturday night grandpa hides eggs for the kids to find on easter sunday.

Advanced Capitals

Capitalize the names of specific things, but don't capitalize general things.

SPECIFIC THINGS	GENERAL THINGS
Africa	continent
Pacific Ocean	ocean
Spain	country
Mount Kilimanjaro	mountain
Paris	city
Main Street	street
Empire State Building	office building
U.S.S. Titanic	ship
Starship Enterprise	spaceship
Magic Shears Hair Salon	beauty parlor
Nikes	tennis shoes
Wheaties	cereal
President Washington	the president
Christianity	religion
Jewish	faith
Episcopal	church

Capitalize the names of ethnic groups, nationalities, and languages:

African-American

Asian

Chinese

Arab

English

Spanish

Capitalize the first word and the important words in the title of a book, movie, poem, painting, etc. (Use italics for the title of a long work, such as a book, movie, magazine, or cd. Use quotation marks around the title of a short work, such as a poem, TV show, article, or song.)

LONG WORKS		SHORT WORKS	
Of Mice and Men	book	"The Lamb"	poem
Titanic	movie	"CSI Miami"	TV show
Better Homes and Gardens	magazine	"Carter wins Nobel Prize"	article
Blues Train	cd	"Fast Train"	song

EXERCISE 9.3 — Advanced Capitals

Correct the capitalization in these sentences.

EXAMPLE: I want to climb Mount Everest.

1. jill lives near the ocean.

2. miss dixon went to tokyo on her vacation.

3. the pacific ocean is larger than the atlantic.

4. most of the people in israel are jewish.

5. on wednesdays i go to my spanish class.

6. columbus sailed to america with the nina, the pinta, and the santa maria.

7. many asian people live in san francisco.

8. in chinatown you can hear lots of people speaking chinese.

9. we could go to an italian restaurant, a mexican restaurant, or a french restaurant.

10. i saw the classic movie *fiddler on the roof* last friday.

Quotation Marks

When you are writing a paragraph, you might want to include some words that people spoke out loud. Put quotation marks around the words that someone spoke. Look at these examples:

- When I walked in the door, everyone yelled, "Surprise!!" They were all wearing party hats and blowing on paper whistles.

- I thought I could install the satellite dish myself, but I should have listened to my girlfriend. "I don't care about saving money. It's too dangerous," she said. I knew she was right when I fell off the ladder and broke my arm.

- I didn't get home until 2 a.m., and my mom said, "Do you know what time it is?" I should have called her, but I didn't want to wake her up. "I haven't been able to sleep because I was so worried," she said.

In each of these examples, the words in quotation marks are the exact words that someone spoke out loud.

Look at the examples below. These sentences don't have the exact words that someone spoke, so quotation marks are not needed:

- When I walked in the door, everyone yelled. They were all wearing party hats and blowing on paper whistles to surprise me.

- I thought I could install the satellite dish myself, but I should have listened to my girlfriend. She didn't care about saving money. She said it was too dangerous. I knew she was right when I fell off the ladder and broke my arm.

- I didn't get home until 2 a.m., and my mom asked me if I knew what time it was. I should have called her, but I didn't want to wake her up. Then she said that she hadn't been able to sleep because she was so worried.

Chapter 10

Homophones

Homophones are words that sound the same but are spelled differently and have different meanings. "Homo" is the Latin word for "same." "Phone" is the Latin word for "sound."

Homophones Part One

ITS	The cat chased ITS ball.
IT'S	IT'S a hot day today.

It's means it is. If you don't mean it is, don't put the apostrophe.

THEIR	My neighbors love THEIR new dog.
THERE	THERE are three frogs in the pond.
	The bathrooms are over THERE.
THEY'RE	Since my neighbors love gardening, THEY'RE planting some new bushes.

Their is possessive. They're means they are. There is used for everything else.

WERE	We WERE stuck in traffic for two hours!
WE'RE	WE'RE going to Florida this summer.

We're means we are. If you don't mean we are, don't use the apostrophe.

YOUR	This is YOUR glass of lemonade.
YOU'RE	YOU'RE not supposed to put the glass on the carpet.

You're means you are. If you don't mean you are, don't use the apostrophe.

THAN	Zack is taller THAN Zoe.
THEN	First we will wash the dishes; THEN we can watch TV.

Use than when you are comparing two things. Use then when you mean time.

TO   I'm going TO the store. I want TO buy some new shoes.

TWO   I will buy TWO pairs of shoes.

TOO   Is that TOO much to buy in one day? Would you like to come TOO?

*Too means **also** or **a lot**. Two means the number 2. Use **to** for everything else.*

EXERCISE 10.1 — Homophones Part One

Circle the correct word.

1. My stomach hurts because I ate (to / two / too) much pizza.

2. I like to go swimming when (its / it's) hot outside.

3. I left my jacket at (your / you're) house.

4. The dog barked and came running (to / two / too) meet me.

5. Why are (their / there / they're) twelve frogs in the bathtub?

6. My car is faster (than / then) your car.

7. Bob and Steve are out washing (their / there / they're) cars.

8. The dog buried (its / it's) bone in the yard.

9. (Were / We're) going to the mountains for the weekend.

10. (Their / There / They're) going to the beach for the weekend.

Homophones Part Two

ARE	We ARE going to the mall.
OUR	This is OUR house.
BUY	I'm saving my money to BUY a car.
BY	I have a night light BY my bed.
HERE	When will Marcus be HERE?
	HERE is that cd I borrowed.
HEAR	Please talk louder. I can't HEAR you.
NO	NO, I don't like tomatoes.
KNOW	Do you KNOW how to bake bread?
RIGHT	At the next intersection, turn RIGHT.
	I believe I got all the answers RIGHT.
WRITE	Denise likes to WRITE poetry.
RODE	I RODE a horse around the corral.
ROAD	Look both ways before you cross the ROAD.
THROUGH	Let's drive THROUGH the park.
THREW	The pitcher THREW a curve ball.
WEEK	My birthday is one WEEK from today.
WEAK	I do push-ups so I'll be strong, not WEAK.
WHERE	WHERE is my hair brush?
WEAR	What should I WEAR today?
WHO'S	Do you know WHO'S going to be at the party?
WHOSE	WHOSE turn is it to set the table?

Who's *means* **who is.** *If you don't mean* **who is,** *don't use the apostrophe.*

EXERCISE 10.2 — Homophones Part Two

Circle the correct word.

1. Why did the chicken cross the (rode / road)?

2. Next (week / weak) is spring break.

3. Candace went to the park (buy / by) the river.

4. I don't (no / know) what to wear today.

5. Two birds are eating at (are / our) bird feeder.

6. (Hear / Here) is the book you were looking for.

7. (Who's / Whose) car should we take?

8. Jessie is (right / write) handed.

9. A bird flew (threw / through) the window into the house.

10. Adam will (where / wear) a tux to the wedding.

Homophones Part Three

ACCEPT	I ACCEPT your apology.
EXCEPT	Joan remembered everything EXCEPT her camera.
BORED	On rainy days, little kids get BORED.
BOARD	We were the last ones to BOARD the plane.
	Steve cut the BOARD in half with his circular saw.
BREAK	When you dry the dishes, be careful not to BREAK one.
	After you work for two hours, you can take a ten minute BREAK.
BRAKE	Hit the BRAKE! You're going too fast!
DESSERT	Finish your mashed turnips or you can't have DESSERT.
DESERT	Cactus grows in the DESERT.
LOOSE	These pants are too LOOSE.
LOSE	Don't LOSE your gloves.
PAST	History teaches stories from the PAST.
PASSED	Oh no! we just PASSED the exit!
	Sally PASSED the class with a B.
PIECE	May I have another PIECE of cake please?
PEACE	While her baby took his nap, Samantha enjoyed an hour of PEACE.
PLANE	Have you ever ridden on an airPLANE?
PLAIN	I don't want a fancy cake; please make me a PLAIN one.
	A big, grassy area is called a PLAIN.
SENSE	That theory just doesn't make any SENSE.
	I have an excellent SENSE of smell.
SINCE	Ever SINCE I won the Academy Award, reporters bother me.
	SINCE I mowed the lawn, I believe you should trim the bushes.
WHETHER	I wonder WHETHER it will rain.
WEATHER	The WEATHER is perfect for a picnic.

EXERCISE 10.3 — Homophones Part Three

Circle the correct word.

1. The bus (passed / past) by while we were running down the sidewalk.

2. If you fall off that ladder, you could (break / brake) your arm.

3. I don't like (plane / plain) yogurt.

4. Tom likes any kind of ice cream (accept / except) spumoni.

5. Camels live in the (dessert / desert).

6. Dan's argument made a lot of (sense / since).

7. Who ate the last (piece / peace) of pie?

8. My shoe laces are too (loose / lose).

9. Kelly enjoyed the cool fall (whether / weather).

10. The meeting was long, and we were so (bored / board).

Chapter 11

The Writing Process

Writing a Paragraph Is Like Baking a Birthday Cake

When kids eat a fancy birthday cake, they don't usually stop to think about all the work that went into making the cake. Baking a cake can be fun, but it also involves a lot of work. The baker has to do many steps in the correct order. Imagine what would happen if the baker put the candles in the cake batter before putting the pans into the oven.

Writing a paragraph is like baking a cake. We can read a paragraph without thinking about how much work went into writing it. Writing a paragraph can be fun, but it also takes time and work. The writer must do many steps in the correct order so that the paragraph will be good.

Steps for Baking a Cake

1. Gather everything you will need: cake mix, vegetable oil, water, eggs, measuring cup, mixing bowl, beater, cake pan, oil spray.

2. Turn on the oven.

3. Put the cake mix into the bowl. Measure the water and vegetable oil and pour them into the bowl. Crack the eggs into the bowl. If you look into the bowl, you will see something kind of gross and disgusting–not something you'd want to eat.

4. Use the beater to mix the ingredients for 2 minutes. Look into the bowl again. It looks much nicer now, all one color and consistency, and it might taste pretty good if you licked the beaters, but eating raw eggs is not a great idea. Your guests wouldn't like this if you served it to them in a bowl.

5. Spray the pan with oil, pour the batter into the pans, and put the pans in the oven. Set the timer and wait. When the timer rings, stick the cake with a toothpick to make sure it is done. Take it out of the oven and put it on a rack to cool. Wait.

    Are you finished? You could serve the cake now, and it would taste good. It will taste better and look much more beautiful if you do a few more steps before serving it.

6. Open a can of frosting and carefully spread it over the sides and top of the cake.

7. For a very fancy cake, use tubes of frosting to make borders, flowers, and other designs on the cake. You can also put candy decorations on the cake.

8. Just before you're ready to serve the cake, stick the candles into the top and light them.

Steps for Writing a Paragraph

1. Gather your ideas: what do you want to say in your paragraph? This step is called *prewriting*. Different prewriting methods include freewriting, clustering, and listing.

2. Turn on your computer or find your paper and pencil. Make yourself comfortable: some people like to listen to music, but others need quiet. Do what works best for you.

3. Write your rough draft. Just type or write down everything you want to say. Don't worry about how messy it looks. At this step you are just throwing everything into the mixing bowl.

   Helpful Hint: When your computer is underlining everything it thinks is wrong, you can get distracted by the lines. Try turning off the spell checker until you finish your rough draft.

4. Do basic revising. Look at your rough draft and see if there is anything that you need to add or to take out. Do you want to move anything around? You're done with basic revising when you said what you wanted to say in an order that makes sense. Now you have a nice draft, but it's not a finished paragraph yet.

5. Now put your paragraph away for a while. This is called incubation. If you take a break from writing, when you come back to your paragraph, you can see it with fresh eyes.

6. Partner revising comes next. Exchange papers with another student and then discuss your paragraphs. Can you add some details? Do you need to take anything out that doesn't belong? Did you tell everything in the correct order, or do you need to move some things around? Is anything confusing? How can you rewrite that part so that the reader can understand easily?

7. Look at the tiny details. Do you have any sentences that are really long? Do you have several short sentences in a row? Try for a nice mixture of sentences — short, medium, and long. Did you use one word over and over again? Try for more variety.

8. Edit your paragraph by fixing any mistakes in spelling, punctuation, or grammar. It is really best to save this step for last. Why waste time on spelling a word when you might end up taking that word out of your paragraph? If you wait till the end to think about spelling, you'll only have to worry about the words that matter.

This comparison of baking a cake and writing a paragraph is an analogy. An analogy is a long comparison of any two things. Can you think of some other activity that could also be compared to writing a paragraph? Try to think of something you know how to do that has several steps that need to be done in a certain order. What would happen if you skipped a step or mixed up the steps?

Don't Skip the First Step!

What's the difference between talking to a friend and writing a paragraph for college?

Imagine that your friend asks you about your vacation. You could talk about the vacation very easily. You wouldn't think much about what you want to say; you would just start talking.

Imagine that your English professor asks you to write a paragraph about your vacation. This would be much harder. You might sit there for quite a while looking at your paper or the computer screen, trying to think what to say and how to say it.

Many students get writers' block because they are trying to do several steps of the writing process at the same time. They are trying to gather ideas, write the rough draft, revise, and edit all at once. Professional writers who write books and movie scripts don't torture themselves that way, so you shouldn't either.

When you know you have to write a paragraph, taking three minutes or so to do prewriting can seem like a waste of time, but really it saves you time and frustration. Once you have gathered your thoughts, you can write your rough draft much more quickly.

There are three main ways to do prewriting: free writing, listing, and clustering. They look different on your paper, but they all have three things in common.

1. Write as fast as you can.

2. Keep writing until the three minutes are up.

3. Don't censor yourself.

Write as fast as you can. Sometimes the best ideas are buried deep in your brain. They tend to pop out when you least expect it. If you write really quickly, an unexpected idea may pop out that you wouldn't have thought of if you were writing at a regular speed or stopping to think before writing.

Keep writing until the three minutes are up. If you can't think of anything to say, don't stop writing. You can write, "I can't think of anything to say," or you can just draw loops on your paper–anything that will keep your pencil moving. If you stop your pencil, you stop the flow of creativity, and the door to your best ideas starts to close again.

Don't censor yourself. *Censor* means to judge ideas as good or bad and only write down the good ones. When you write really quickly without stopping, many of the ideas you write down will be not that good. That's ok. You only need one good idea, and sometimes you have to write twenty bad ideas before the good one pops out unexpectedly. Whatever comes to mind, just write it down, no matter how silly it is. (You can always shred the paper later if you write something really embarrassing!)

Freewriting

Freewriting (also called brainstorming) looks like a paragraph on the page. You write on the lines, but you DON'T think about spelling or anything else. Just write as quickly as you can without stopping for three minutes. Whatever comes to mind, write it down. Don't go back and fix or change anything. Keep going full steam ahead. Your writing might come out as sentences or maybe not. It doesn't matter.

> What do I want to rite about? Umm where have I been on vacation? The beach mountains Disney world. The beach wold be good. Umm I could tell about swimming and skiing. Fishing seafood restaurants kids can dig in the sand, make sandcassles you can get a tan but don't get burned. Relaxing, fun

When the three minutes are up, read what you wrote. If your freewriting is full of mistakes, that means you did it correctly!

A freewrite is not the same thing as a rough draft. A rough draft is written a little more slowly and is not quite so messy. But practicing freewriting helps you separate the creative parts of writing (gathering ideas, writing the rough draft) from the analytical parts (revising and editing). Once you get the hang of writing without trying to revise and edit at the same time, you will be able to write rough drafts much more quickly and easily.

Listing

Listing is just like freewriting except that the ideas are written as a list rather than a paragraph. Sometimes you may write just one word for each idea, or some of your ideas might be several words or even a sentence. If you run out of things to say, draw loops or anything to keep your pencil moving on the page.

Listing can also be helpful after you have your topic and you need to think about what you want to say about it. Write quickly, just like with freewriting. If something comes to mind that doesn't really relate to your topic, don't censor it. Write that idea down. You can go back later and cross out the ideas you don't want to use in your paragraph. Don't worry about the order of your ideas on this list. You can go back later and re-write the list in a logical order.

> Beach vacation
> Swimming
> Fishin
> Sun tan, don't get burned though
> Hotel has a swimming pool
> Umm
> Umm
> What else?
> Outdoor concerts in summer?
> Volleyball
> jetski

Clustering

Clustering is like listing because most of your ideas are written as just one word or a couple of words rather than as sentences. Clustering is different from listing because you can write things anywhere on the page and draw lines to connect ideas.

Clustering is most often used after you have a topic in mind. You can write your topic in the center of the page and then think of things you could say about your topic and write them all over the page. One idea might lead to another, and you can draw lines to connect your train of thought. Don't let that slow you down though. Write quickly and don't censor yourself. If you can't think of anything to say, draw circles all over the page to keep your pencil moving.

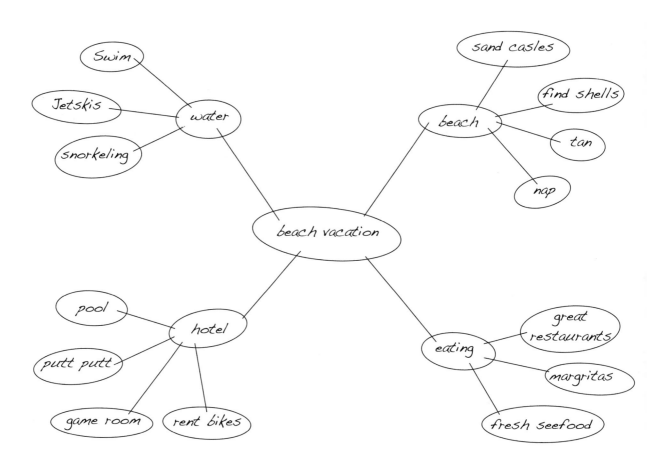

One More Method — Talking

If you just can't write anything down, try talking to another student about the assignment. Your partner may be able to ask you some questions that will get your juices flowing. Try answering these basic questions: *who, what, why, where, when, how?* If you have a topic in mind but you can't start writing, try telling your partner about the topic and then writing down what you said. Once the words start flowing out of your mouth, they will flow onto the paper more easily.

EXERCISE 11.1 — Gathering Ideas

What suggestions could you give to a student who is having these problems? Would freewriting, listing, clustering, or talking help? Do you have other suggestions or advice?

1. "Every time I begin to write I can't think of anything to say. It takes me forever to write a sentence, and then I feel like I should just start all over."

2. "I finished my rough draft, but it's too short, and I just don't know what else to say."

3. "My instructor has asked me to write about a special event in my life. I've had several and don't know which one to pick."

4. "I know a lot about the topic my instructor wants me to write about. I just don't know how to put my ideas together."

5. "I know what I want to write about. I just need to figure out how to get started."

6. "I have writer's block. I can't think of anything to write."

Purpose and Audience

> *milk*
> *eggs*
> *bread*
> *frozen pizza*
> *diapers*
> *formula*
> *wet wipes*
> *cat food*

What is this writing?
Who probably wrote it?
Who did the author expect to read it (the audience)?
What was the author's purpose for writing this list?

> tos ttyl

Where would you see a message like this?
Who probably wrote this message?
Who did the author expect to read it (the audience)?
What was the author's purpose for writing this message?

> **Garments left for**
> **more than 30 days**
> **will be donated**
> **to a local charity**

Where would you see a sign like this?
Who probably wrote this sign?
Who did the author expect to read it (the audience)?
What was the author's purpose for writing it?

> Each employee's hands must be washed thoroughly
> using soap, warm water, and a sanitary towel or approved hand drying device
> before beginning work and after each visit to the toilet.

Where would you see a sign like this?
Who probably wrote the sign?
Who did the author expect to read it (the audience)?
What was the author's purpose for writing it?

> To receive an original driver license in North Carolina, you must bring at least two acceptable forms of identification. At least one must reflect your full name, including your middle name. If both forms of identification have only a middle initial, and your birth certificate is not one of the forms of identification you are presenting, you must present certified documentation indicating the same. At least one form of identification must include your date of birth. You must complete and pass the written, sign, and vision tests. Proof of residency and liability insurance on your car are required in addition to your Social Security card. If you are not eligible for a Social Security card, you must provide documentation issued by the United States Government indicating legal presence.

Where would you find this information?
Who probably wrote this?
Who did the author expect to read it (the audience)?
What was the author's purpose for writing it?

> What did the number 0 say to the number 8?
> Nice belt!

Where would you see this?
Who probably wrote it?
Who did the author expect to read it (the audience)?
What was the author's purpose for writing it?

Every piece of writing has a **purpose** and an **audience**.

Purpose: your reason for writing

Audience: the person you are writing to

Different Types of Purposes

To give *information* or *explain* something

Most of the writing we do for college and at work is informative. Your purpose is to give correct information and explain everything clearly so that your reader can understand it easily.

The shopping list, text message, laundry sign, and driver's license information are all examples of this kind of writing.

What other kinds writing (for college, work, and everyday life) can you think of that fit this purpose?

To *persuade*

When you write persuasion, your purpose is to get someone to do something. Most of the commercials and advertisements that we see are trying to persuade us to buy something or do something or vote for someone.

The hand washing sign is trying to get employees to wash their hands. The laundry sign is partly persuasion because the laundry owner wants people to pick up their clothes within thirty days.

What other kinds of writing (for college, work, and everyday life) can you think of that fit this purpose?

To *entertain*

The purpose of entertainment is to give the reader an enjoyable experience. Entertaining writing usually tells a story. The TV shows and movies we watch for entertainment all started out as writing. Entertainment doesn't always mean happy though. Movies can be funny, but they can also be scary, exciting, or sad. In the best movies, we forget that we're sitting in a movie theater and get totally caught up in the story. You can do the same thing when you write a story.

The joke about the number 0 is entertaining, of course. What other kinds of writing (for college, work, or everyday life) can you think of that fit this purpose?

To *discover* something

Just like we can talk about a question or problem to figure it out, we can also write to figure things out or to think about things. For college, you might write a paragraph answering a question like, "If you won a million dollars in the lottery, what would you do?" There isn't a right or wrong answer to this question. Each person's answer will be different. You just imagine winning the lottery and write about what you would do.

Another good use for discovery writing is as a first step in solving a problem. If you need to write a paragraph for college but don't know what to say, you could start by writing to yourself and thinking about the topic on paper. Discovery writing can also be helpful at work and in everyday life. What kinds of situations (for college, work, or everyday life) could you use discovery writing for?

Different Types of Audiences

If you're writing a text message to a friend, you don't need to worry about spelling. But if your audience is your college professor, spelling will matter a lot.

Here are some questions to ask yourself about your audience:

How formal should I be? Is it ok to use slang or not?

How old is the reader? Can I explain the information quickly, or do I need to go slowly?

What does the reader already know? Will I need to explain what some words mean?

What are the reader's expectations?

The police lieutenant expects police reports to be written a certain way.

The college professor expects a research paper to have correct documentation.

EXERCISE 11.2 — Audience

Discuss each of the following writing tasks. How would you change what you write based on the audience?

Directions for changing the ringtone on a cell phone

1. Young adult who has used several different cell phones and spends at least an hour on-line every day.

2. Senior citizen who has never used a cell phone before and has no experience with computers at all.

Telling how another driver ran a red light and hit your car

1. Your friend

2. Your boss to explain why you were late for work

3. The police officer filling out the accident report

Persuading someone not to feed the dog scraps from the table

1. Your spouse

2. Your father or mother

3. Your child

Point and Support

A good paragraph makes a point and then supports or proves the point. The first sentence of your paragraph is called the **topic sentence**. This is where you make your point.

Make sure that the point (main idea) of your paragraph is something that needs to be proved.

> Iguanas are reptiles.

This sentence doesn't need to be proved. It is a fact. If this is your topic sentence, you will have trouble writing the rest of the paragraph.

> Iguanas make good pets.

The second sentence is an opinion because your reader might disagree. This is a good topic sentence because there are plenty of things you could say to support it or prove it.

Why is an iguana a good pet? What are your reasons?

> Reason #1: Iguanas don't have fur.
> Reason #2: They don't bark or make noise.
> Reason #3: They live in a cage.
> Reason #4: They don't need a lot of care.
> Reason #5: They are inexpensive.

These are five good reasons why iguanas make good pets. But you can't just have a list of reasons as your paragraph. You need to explain the reasons and give some details.

Topic Sentence: Iguanas make good pets.

Reason #1:   Iguanas don't have fur.

    Detail: You won't have fur all over your house and clothes.

    Detail: Iguanas are good for people with allergies.

    Detail: They shed their skin every few months, and it is easy to pick up the skin and throw it away.

Reason #2:   They don't bark or make noise.

    Detail: You never have to worry about bothering your neighbors.

    Detail: You don't have to listen to annoying barking, yowling, or whining.

Reason #3:   They live in a cage.

    Detail: You will never have to clean up accidents on the rug

    Detail: All the mess stays in the cage so your house stays clean.

    Detail: It's easy to clean the cage every two weeks or so.

Reason #4:   They don't need a lot of care.

    Detail: Iguanas don't need a lot of exercise.

    Detail: If you're busy, you can mostly leave the iguana alone.

    Detail: If you go on vacation, it's easy to get someone to fill their food and water every few days.

Reason #5:   They are inexpensive.

    Detail: The cage set up can be elaborate, or you can spend only about $100.

    Detail: You can buy a small iguana for about $50.

    Detail: The food is inexpensive–about $10 per month.

    Detail: They almost never need veterinary care.

This plan would make a great paragraph. It has strong reasons and details that support and prove the point.

A list of what is written in a paragraph (or essay) is called an **outline**. Writing an outline of your paragraph can be a good way to plan what you want to say.

Enough Reasons

To prove or support your topic sentence, make sure you have enough reasons. If you only have one reason why iguanas make good pets, your reader may not be convinced:

Iguanas make good pets. They don't have fur, so you won't have fur all over your house and clothes. Many people are allergic to animal fur, so iguanas are good pets for people with allergies. Like most reptiles, they shed their skin every few months, but it is easy to pick up the skin and throw it away.

A reader who doesn't mind animal fur wouldn't choose an iguana if the only reason you give is that it doesn't have fur.

EXERCISE 11.3 — Enough Reasons

Fill in the blanks to give more support or reasons for these topic sentences:

1. **Dogs make good pets**

    Provide protection

    _____

    _____

    _____

2. **Cats make good pets.**

    Not too noisy

    _____

    _____

    _____

3. **Owning a car is expensive.**

    Insurance

    _____

    _____

    _____

4. **Working and going to school is hard**

    Don't get enough sleep

    _____

    _____

    _____

5. **Florida is a great place for a vacation.**

    Theme parks

    _____

    _____

    _____

6. **Lady Gaga is a controversial performer.**

    Costumes

    _____

    _____

    _____

Strong, Specific Details

Just as the reasons support the topic sentence, the details support the reasons. A good paragraph has details that are specific, not general.

General: Iguanas are clean.

Specific: Iguanas don't shed fur.

EXERCISE 11.4 — Specific Details

Circle the detail that is more specific.

1. The burgers were bad, the fries were bad, and the milkshakes were bad.
   The burgers were cold, the fries were greasy, and the milkshakes were watery.

2. He belched loudly and picked his nose.
   He had bad manners.

3. I waited a long time to register for classes.
   I waited three hours to register for classes.

4. My roommate leaves her dirty clothes all over the apartment.
   My roommate is messy.

5. I have lots of stuff to do today.
   I have to go to school, go to work, and do grocery shopping today.

6. I had a rough day at work today.
   Two people called in sick, and I didn't get my break.

7. Suzanne's face turned red, and she ran out of the room.
   Suzanne got upset.

8. The movie was great.
   The movie had lots of action scenes and special effects.

9. These shoes pinch my toes.
   These shoes are uncomfortable.

10. Professor Smith is really demanding.
    Professor Smith assigns fifty pages of reading each night.

EXERCISE 11.5 — Writing Specific Details

Rewrite each sentence to make it more specific.

1. My boss is a *jerk*.

   _____

2. Candace is *beautiful*.

   _____

3. The roller coaster was *exciting*.

   _____

4. The dress looked *cheap*.

   _____

5. I didn't feel *good*.

   _____

6. George's commute is *terrible*.

   _____

7. Her car is a piece of *junk*.

   _____

8. There was *lots of stuff* in the backseat of the car.

   _____

9. That customer was *annoying*.

   _____

10. This course is really *hard*.

   _____

Relevant Support

Make sure that the reasons and details you give are **relevant.** This means that they actually go with your topic. Which two of the reasons below are not relevant to the topic sentence?

Topic Sentence: Iguanas make good pets.

> Reason #1:   Iguanas don't have fur.
> Reason #2:   Iguanas aren't very friendly.
> Reason #3:   They live in a cage.
> Reason #4:   Hamsters also live in a cage.
> Reason #5:   Iguanas are inexpensive.

Reason #2 is something bad about iguanas. This reason does not help prove to the reader that they make good pets. Reason #4 isn't even about iguanas. It doesn't belong in this paragraph.

EXERCISE 11.6 — Relevant Support

Circle the support that is not relevant, that doesn't belong.

Burger King is a good place to work.
Flexible hours
Good pay
Don't get free food
Opportunity to advance

The restaurant was terrible.
Cute, friendly waiter
Bad food
Dirty silverware
High prices

Gerbils make good pets.
Cats will eat them
Quiet
Inexpensive
Fun to watch

I had fun at the fair.
Won a stuffed animal at ring toss
Saw interesting exhibits
Got sick on the roller coaster
Ate cotton candy and corn dogs

Leonardo DiCaprio is a versatile actor.
Romantic movies
Adventure movies
Dramas
Charity work

My blind date was a disaster.
I was late for work that morning.
My date showed up 20 minutes late.
He was a foot shorter than me.
He chewed with his mouth open.

My apartment is a dump.
Stained carpet
Leaky faucets
Great view
Peeling paint

My blind date was wonderful.
He was good-looking.
He opened the car door for me.
He was charming and funny.
He is allergic to shellfish.

Organization/Structure

When you write your paragraph, think about how you want to arrange all your reasons and your details. Group things together that go together.

Imagine how hard it would be to read a paragraph in which everything was scrambled together:

Topic Sentence: Iguanas make good pets.

They almost never need veterinary care.

You will never have to clean up accidents on the rug.

If you're busy, you can mostly leave the iguana alone.

They shed their skin every few months, and it is easy to pick up the skin and throw it away.

They don't need a lot of care.

They live in a cage.

They don't bark or make noise.

You can buy a small iguana for about $50.

You don't have to listen to annoying barking, yowling, or whining.

You won't have fur all over your house and clothes.

Iguanas are good for people with allergies.

They are inexpensive

It's easy to clean the cage every two weeks or so.

Iguanas don't have fur.

Iguanas don't need a lot of exercise.

If you go on vacation, it's easy to get someone to fill their food and water every few days.

You never have to worry about bothering your neighbors.

The cage set up can be elaborate, or you can spend only about $100.

All the mess stays in the cage so your house stays clean.

The food is inexpensive — about $10 per month.

EXERCISE 11.7 — Organization

Compare the list of reasons and details above to the organized outline on page 95.

Write the number 1, 2, 3, 4, or 5 beside each item on this list to show which details go with each reason.

EXERCISE 11.8 — Organization

Look at this scrambled list of reasons and details. Re-write the items on the list in the blanks to create an organized outline.

Topic Sentence: Sage is a great restaurant.

The chocolate mousse cake is rich and creamy.

The lights are dim and they have candles on the tables.

The food is delicious.

The chef will come to the table and ask how you like the food.

All the vegetables are fresh and locally grown.

Soft music plays in the background.

The atmosphere is relaxing.

The hostess gives me my favorite table.

The chef uses fresh herbs for seasoning.

The servers are friendly and very quick.

The staff is friendly.

The chairs are big and comfortable.

Topic Sentence: Sage is a great restaurant.

Reason #1 _____

    Detail _____

    Detail _____

    Detail _____

Reason #2 _____

    Detail _____

    Detail _____

    Detail _____

Reason #3 _____

    Detail _____

    Detail _____

    Detail _____

EXERCISE 11.9 — Outlining

Read this paragraph and then fill in the blanks of the outline:

Florida is a wonderful place to go on vacation. First, if you want to relax, Florida has plenty of options. The beaches are beautiful for taking walks at sunset or for getting a tan. If you like to fish, you can spend all day sitting on a pier and chatting with others while you try to catch your dinner. Lying in a hammock between two palm trees and reading a book is the ultimate relaxation, especially with the gentle breeze blowing and the sound of the waves in the distance. Second, Florida offers lots of active adventures. You can snorkel or scuba dive and explore a coral reef. You can try water skiing or riding a jet ski. Since the weather is nice all year round, you can play outdoor sports like baseball or frisbee in the middle of winter. Finally, Florida has the world's best theme parks. Disney World is huge, and it would take you a week to see everything. For animal lovers, Sea World offers a chance to learn about all kinds of water animals and even see amazing performances by trained whales. Movie lovers will enjoy Universal Studios where you can see how movies are made and go on rides based on favorite movies. No matter what kind of vacation you want, you can have a great time in Florida.

Topic Sentence: _____

    Reason #1 _____

        Detail _____

        Detail _____

        Detail _____

    Reason #2 _____

        Detail _____

        Detail _____

        Detail _____

    Reason #3 _____

        Detail _____

        Detail _____

        Detail _____

Conclusion Sentence* _____

*A conclusion sentence makes your paragraph sound finished. A good conclusion sentence may be similar to the topic sentence (the first sentence), but don't just copy the topic sentence. Write a new sentence.

Transitions

There are two ways to arrange the information in your paragraph. You can use **time order** or **list order**. No matter which order you use, put transition words between the reasons or main parts of your paragraph. Your paragraph will sound better and be easier for the reader to understand.

When you use **time order**, you tell things in the same order that they happened. This is perfect for telling a story or for explaining the steps of how to do something. For example, if you're giving directions for changing a tire, you have to give the steps in the correct order. The reader needs to jack up the car before trying to take off the flat tire.

Transitions for a time order paragraph include words like *first, second, third, next, after, while, during, before, later, finally, last.*

Use **list order** when your reasons and details could be arranged in any order. The paragraphs about iguanas and about Florida are examples of list order. The reasons could be rearranged and the paragraph would still sound fine.

Here is the original order for the paragraph about iguanas:

Iguanas don't have fur.

They don't bark or make noise.

They live in a cage.

They don't need a lot of exercise.

They are inexpensive.

Here is another good way of arranging the reasons:

Iguanas are inexpensive.

They live in a cage.

They don't have fur.

They don't need a lot of exercise.

They don't bark or make noise.

Transitions for a list order paragraph include words like *one, first, another, next, second, last, also.* (Some transition words can be used for list order or for time order.)

Practice with Time Order Transitions

EXERCISE 11.10 — Finding Time Order Transitions

Circle the transition words in this paragraph:

Jody had a terrible day at school. First, the traffic seemed even worse than usual, and she couldn't find a parking place. She had to park in the grass lot which was muddy from a week of rain. Even though she nearly ran to her class, she was ten minutes late, and the professor gave her a dirty look. Then there was a pop quiz, and Jody couldn't find a pen or pencil. When the class ended, Jody went to the bathroom. She was horrified when she looked in the mirror and saw that her shirt was buttoned up the wrong way. "The cute guy who sits behind me must think I'm a slob," she thought. Later, when she went to the café for lunch, the pizza was sold out, so Jody had to eat a dried out corn dog. Finally, in her last class the professor assigned a five page essay that was due the next day. "There goes my chance for relaxing tonight," Jamie told her friend Kate. As she walked to her car, Jamie tried to cheer up by telling herself that tomorrow would have to be a much better day.

EXERCISE 11.11 — Writing Time Order Transitions

Fill in the blanks with transition words:

It is easy to change a flat tire if you follow these steps. _____ pull off the road onto a flat area. _____ take the tire iron out of the trunk and use it to pry off the wheel cover. Use the other end of the tire iron to loosen the nuts, but don't take them all the way off. _____ get the jack out of the trunk and put it under the frame of the car near the flat tire. Be sure the jack is on a solid, flat surface. Jack up the car until the flat tire is up off the ground. _____ take off the nuts and put them in the wheel cover so they don't roll away. Lift off the flat tire. _____ put the spare tire onto the bolts. Screw on the nuts until they are snug but not tight. _____ lower the jack and remove it from under the car. Use the tire iron to tighten all the nuts. _____ put the tools, wheel cover, and flat tire in your trunk, and you are good to go. You just saved a lot of money by changing your own tire.

Practice with List Order Transitions

EXERCISE 11.12 — Finding List Order Transitions

Circle the transition words in this paragraph:

Florida is wonderful place to go on vacation. First, if you want to relax, Florida has plenty of options. The beaches are beautiful for taking walks at sunset or for getting a tan. If you like to fish, you can spend all day sitting on a pier and chatting with others while you try to catch your dinner. Lying in a hammock between two palm trees and reading a book is the ultimate relaxation, especially with the gentle breeze blowing and the sound of the waves in the distance. Second, Florida offers lots of active adventures. You can snorkel or scuba dive and explore a coral reef. You can try water skiing or riding a jet ski. Since the weather is nice all year round, you can play outdoor sports like baseball or frisbee in the middle of winter. Finally, Florida has the world's best theme parks. Disney World is huge, and it would take you a week to see everything. For animal lovers, Sea World offers a chance to learn about all kinds of water animals and even see amazing performances by trained whales. Movie lovers will enjoy Universal Studios where you can see how movies are made and go on rides based on favorite movies. No matter what kind of vacation you want, you can have a great time in Florida.

EXERCISE 11.13 — Writing List Order Transitions

Fill in the blanks with transition words:

Sage is a great restaurant. _____ the food is delicious. All the vegetables are fresh and locally grown, so the salads are crisp and the side dishes are succulent. The chef uses fresh herbs for seasoning which give a unique flavor to all the dishes. I always save room for dessert because the chocolate mousse cake is rich and creamy. _____ the restaurant's atmosphere is relaxing. Soft music plays in the background and candles flicker in the dim light. As soon as I sink into one of the big comfortable chairs, my whole body relaxes. _____ the staff is professional and friendly. When we walk in the door, the hostess remembers us and takes us to our favorite table. All the servers are quick to take our order and bring our food, but they never make us feel rushed about eating. Many times the chef has come to our table to ask how everything tastes. Whenever I'm tired, stressed, and don't feel like cooking, I go to Sage for a delicious, relaxing meal.

FAQ — Frequently Asked Questions

"Does the topic sentence have to come first?"

Well, no, but it's usually best to put it first. Sometimes you may have a sentence that leads in to the topic sentence, and your topic sentence is the second sentence. That's fine too. You probably don't want it in the middle though.

"How many reasons do I need?"

It depends on the topic you're writing about, but it's usually good to have at least three.

"Does it matter what order I put things in?"

If you're writing a story, you would tell things in the order in which they happened. If you're not writing a story, you'll want to put similar things together, but other than that, you can decide what order to put your reasons and what order to put the details for each reason. Just put everything in an order that you think will sound good. Saving your best reason for last can work well.

"Do I need three details for every reason?"

No. For some reasons you may have only one or two details. For other reasons you may have three or four or more.

"What about the conclusion sentence?"

Every paragraph should have a conclusion sentence so it sounds finished. The conclusion sentence sums up everything you've said. It often has a similar meaning to your topic sentence, but it should be a different sentence. Don't just copy your topic sentence again at the end.

Chapter 12

Writing Different Kinds of Paragraphs

Narration — Telling a Story

People tell stories all the time. They tell their family what happened at work or school that day. They tell a friend what happened at a football game. They tell their roommate what happened on a date. When you tell a story, you are telling **what happened**.

Topic Sentence: the first sentence of your paragraph should tell the point or main idea of the story. "Winning the state championship in football was the greatest night of my life."

Structure/Organization: Tell what happened from the beginning to the end. This is called time order or chronological order. Use transition words like "first," "next," "then," "later," "finally."

Details: Try to tell your story so that the reader feels like he or she is right there as it's happening. This means that you must *give plenty of details*. If you write a paragraph about four years of playing high school football, you won't have room to give any details. Instead, write about the most important or exciting day or hour of the story, like one big game or one big play. Don't give more background information than the reader needs.

Thinking of Ideas (Invention) for Your Narrative Paragraph

Think back over your life, from when you were a little child until now. Make a list of all the important, interesting, or funny events in your life. Write down everything you can remember.

> nearly drowning in the ocean — 8 years old
> moving from Missouri to Florida — 7 years old
> singing my first concert in choir — 7th grade
> bullies in middle school
> when I broke my wrist
> being in plays in high school
> homecoming senior year
> high school graduation
> getting married
> car accident, going to hospital in an ambulance

Now look through your list and choose your two favorite events, the two stories that seem like they would be interesting to write about. Then do a three minute freewrite for each of your two events. When you free write, don't worry about spelling or if it sounds right. Just write as fast as you can. Ask yourself, "If I chose this topic for my paragraph, what would I want to tell?" Try to write without stopping for three minutes. Then stop, take a breath, and do a free write for the second idea. After you have finished, you will have spent only 6 minutes, but you will know which idea was easiest and most fun to write about.

Your free write doesn't take the place of your rough draft, but the rough draft will be easier to write since you already have your thoughts flowing. After you write the rough draft, put your story away for a while so that you can see it with fresh eyes when you start to revise.

Rough Draft of a Narrative Paragraph

I played football all through high school. My team was really good. In my sophomore and senior year we were in the playoffs. In my sophomore year, we lost in the quarter finals because our best wide receiver sprained his ankle. I was the second receiver, and I dropped the ball three times. We lost that game. It was a big disappointment to everybody on the team. Then my junior year we had a pretty good season, but we didn't make it to the playoffs. My senior year we had a great season. We lost only one game in the regular season. We were so excited about going to the playoffs. When we made it to the championship game, we were so excited. We were not going to lose this time. The game was so exciting. I scored a touchdown with only three minutes left, and we won. This was the greatest game of my life, a night I will never forget.

Things to Think About When You Revise

1. Does the topic sentence (first sentence) of your paragraph tell the point or main idea of the story?

2. How long of a time period does your story cover? Did you focus on the most important and exciting moments without giving too much background information?

3. Did you tell what happened in the order that it happened?

4. What kinds of details did you give so that the reader feels like he or she is right there in the middle of the story? Can you add any more details? What did you see, hear, feel?

5. Can you add any dialogue in your story? Dialogue is words that people speak out loud. See page 76 for information on how to write dialogue.

6. Does your last sentence give the story a feeling of conclusion?

After Revision

Winning the state championship in football was the greatest night of my life. In the first half, the team members were nervous. We couldn't focus, so we kept making mistakes. We had two penalties for offsides, and our quarterback got sacked. I was the wide receiver, and I dropped a ball that should have been a touch down. At half time we were trailing 7 to 14. We went into the locker room, and the head coach told us, "We have worked hard all season to get to this game. Let's start acting like the champions we are. I want to bring home that trophy!" In the second half, we settled down and started to score points. The score was tied at 21 to 21 with three minutes left on the clock. We had the ball, and the quarterback called, "Twenty-two, sixteen, thirty-four, hut hut hut!" This was my big play. I got around the linesman and ran up the field as fast as I could until I crossed the goal line. Then I turned and looked for the ball. It was coming right at me in a beautiful arch. I raised my hands and jumped. My hands grabbed the ball, and this time I held on tight. I saw the referee's arms go up, and the crowd screamed. All my teammates ran up and started punching me because they were so happy. I had scored the winning touchdown. This was a night I will never forget.

Compare this revised paragraph to the rough draft.

1.   What did the author take out of the rough draft?

2.   How long of a time period does this paragraph cover compared to the rough draft?

3.   What details did the author add to show the reader what he saw, heard, and felt?

Inspiration

"Out, Out —"
Robert Frost (1874–1963)

The buzz saw snarled and rattled in the yard   *buzz saw* — chain saw
And made dust and dropped stove-length sticks of wood,
Sweet-scented stuff when the breeze drew across it.
And from there those that lifted eyes could count
Five mountain ranges one behind the other
Under the sunset far into Vermont.
And the saw snarled and rattled, snarled and rattled,
As it ran light, or had to bear a load.
And nothing happened: day was all but done.
Call it a day, I wish they might have said
To please the boy by giving him the half hour
That a boy counts so much when saved from work.
His sister stood beside him in her apron
To tell them 'Supper.' At the word, the saw,
As if to prove saws know what supper meant,
Leaped out at the boy's hand, or seemed to leap —
He must have given the hand. However it was,
Neither refused the meeting. But the hand!   *Neither refused the meeting* —
The boy's first outcry was a rueful laugh,   the saw has cut off his hand
As he swung toward them holding up the hand
Half in appeal, but half as if to keep
The life from spilling. Then the boy saw all —
Since he was old enough to know, big boy
Doing a man's work, though a child at heart —
He saw all was spoiled. 'Don't let him cut my hand off —
The doctor, when he comes. Don't let him, sister!'
So. But the hand was gone already.
The doctor put him in the dark of ether.   *ether* — an old-fashioned
He lay and puffed his lips out with his breath.   anesthesia
And then — the watcher at his pulse took fright.
No one believed. They listened to his heart.
Little — less — nothing! — and that ended it.
No more to build on there. And they, since they
Were not the one dead, turned to their affairs.

The title of this poem comes from Shakespeare's famous play *MacBeth*. The character MacBeth knows he will die soon in battle, and he is talking to himself about how fragile life is and how easily it can end, just like blowing out a candle.

   Out, out, brief candle! / Life's but a walking shadow, a poor player, / That struts and frets his hour upon the stage, / And then is heard no more.

Exemplification — Giving Examples

There are many ways you can write a paragraph that gives an example. For this assignment, you will write a paragraph that gives advice. You will tell a story that gives an example of the advice.

Parents often use stories to give advice to their children. If a parent says, "Look both ways before you cross the street," the child might forget that advice. When the parent tells a story about a child who ran into the street and got hit by a car, the child is more likely to remember and follow the advice.

Advice paragraphs are not just for children though. Adults use stories to give advice to each other. Another student might tell you, "Don't wait until the last minute to register for your classes." The student might go on to tell you a story about her first semester of college when she tried to register the day before classes began and all the classes she needed were full.

Your paragraph can be serious or funny depending on the lesson you are teaching and the story you tell.

Topic Sentence: The first sentence of your paragraph should give the advice which your story will teach. "Don't wait until the last minute to register for your classes."

Structure/Organization: After the topic sentence, tell the story in the order that things happened. This is called time order or chronological order. Use transition words like "first," "next," "then," "later," "finally."

Details: Explain everything clearly so that the reader understands exactly what happened and why. Focus on the most important part of the story; don't give more background information than the reader needs. Give details of what you saw, heard, and felt, so the reader feels like he or she is right in the middle of the story.

Thinking of Ideas (Invention) for Your Exemplification Paragraph

There are two ways you can think of ideas for this paragraph. One way is to think back over your life and make a list of all the events which could be used for giving advice.

> nearly drowning in the ocean — always wear a life jacket
> when I fell off my bike — always wear a helmet
> when I went on a blind date — get honest info about
>   someone before a blind date

Another way to get ideas is to start with the advice and then to think of a story that would be a good example. The story doesn't have to be about you. It can be about another person as long as you know the story well and can give plenty of details.

It isn't what you know, it's who you know.

Out of sight is out of mind.

Absence makes the heart grow fonder.

Procrastination is the thief of time.

Never loan money to a friend.

Listen to your gut.

You get what you pay for.

If something seems too good to be true, it probably is.

Good things come to those who wait.

You make your own good luck.

Don't look a gift horse in the mouth.

Actions speak louder than words.

Haste makes waste.

A fool and his/her money are soon parted.

If it isn't broken, don't fix it.

What goes around, comes around.

When you have a topic in mind, do a three minute freewrite about the story. When you free write, don't worry about spelling or if it sounds right. Just write as fast as you can. Ask yourself, "If I chose this topic for my paragraph, what would I want to tell?" Try to write without stopping for three minutes. After you have finished, you will know if this idea will work as a paragraph and if you really want to write about it.

Your free write doesn't take the place of your rough draft, but the rough draft will be easier to write since you already have your thoughts flowing. After you write the rough draft, put your paragraph away for a while so that you can see it with fresh eyes when you start to revise.

Things to Think About When You Revise

1. Does the topic sentence (first sentence) of your paragraph give the advice that your story is teaching?

2. Did you focus on the most important and exciting moments of the story without giving too much background information?

3. Did you tell what happened in the order that things happened?

4. What kinds of details did you give so that the reader feels like he or she is right there in the middle of the story? Can you add any more details? What did you see, hear, feel?

5. Can you include any dialogue in your story? Dialogue is words that people speak out loud. See page 76 for information on how to write dialogue.

6. Does your last sentence give the story a feeling of conclusion?

Funny Exemplification Paragraph

When you try on clothing, be sure it fits when you are sitting down. When my fiancé and I started planning our wedding, I decided to sew my own wedding dress to save money. I took my measurements and bought a pattern that was the right size. While I was sewing it, I tried the dress on many times, and it fit me perfectly. When I finished it, the dress looked beautiful. I never thought about sitting down to make sure the dress was comfortable when I was sitting. During the wedding and the photographs, I was standing up, and everything was fine. Then we went to the reception. When I sat down at the table to eat lunch, the waistband of the dress squeezed my stomach, and it was really uncomfortable. At first I thought the waistband of my panty hose was too tight. I went to the bathroom and pulled the panty hose down a little bit so the waistband was around my hips. When I went back to the table and sat down again, I realized that it was the dress that was too tight. I couldn't do anything about that, so I just endured the pain. I could hardly eat lunch, and I was glad when the meal was over and I could stand up again to eat cake. I had a beautiful wedding and a beautiful dress, and all the guests said the food was delicious. All I knew was that after this experience, I would always be sure to sit down when trying on clothes.

Serious Exemplification Paragraph

Always wear your seat belt. I learned this lesson two years ago. My cousin and I were driving home from the mall on a summer afternoon. The sky was sunny, there was no ice or water on the road, and there wasn't much traffic. Even though the driving conditions were very safe, my cousin and I both had our seat belts on just out of habit. We were almost home when a car ran through a red light and smashed into the passenger side of the car where I was sitting. Our car rolled over twice and then slid into the ditch and landed on the roof. I banged my head on the windshield and passed out. The next thing I knew, the EMT was saying, "Just relax. I'm going to hold your head still while Josh cuts the seat belt so we can get you out." Then I passed out again, and when I woke up, I was lying in a hospital bed. My mom and dad and my two sisters were standing around the bed. When I opened my eyes, my mom said, "She's awake! She's awake! Go get the nurse!" Then my family told me that I had been unconscious for two days. They said I had gone through four hours of surgery to repair my lung after a broken rib had torn it. I also had a brain injury and two broken legs. The doctors had said I had a 30% chance of surviving the accident. If I hadn't been wearing a seatbelt, I would have died instantly. Wearing a seatbelt can be a hassle, but it's really worth it. A seatbelt could save your life just like it saved mine.

Process Analysis — Telling the Steps

In this paragraph your **purpose** is to give clear, step-by-step directions about how to do something. Your **audience** is a person who has never done this thing before. Most of the directions that we read in our every-day lives are written for someone who already knows a lot about the topic.

Yellow Cake

1 cup all-purpose flour
3/4 cup white sugar
1/4 cup butter, softened
1/2 cup milk
2 teaspoons baking powder
1/2 teaspoon salt
1 teaspoon vanilla extract
2 whole eggs

Preheat oven to 350 degrees F. Grease and flour pans. Mix flour, baking powder and salt; set aside.

In large bowl, cream sugar and butter until light and fluffy. Add eggs one at a time, beating thoroughly after each addition. Add flour mixture alternately with milk, beating just to combine. Finally, stir in vanilla. Pour batter into prepared pan.

Bake at 350 degrees F (175 degrees C) for 40 to 45 minutes, or until toothpick comes out clean.

If you already know how to bake a cake, following these directions will be easy. But if you have never baked a cake before, it will be hard. The author has left out many words (especially THE and A) and hasn't explained things very clearly.

How soft should the butter be? Can I microwave it to soften it?
What does it mean to "cream sugar and butter until light and fluffy"?
The batter is really thick and won't pour. How do I get it into the pans?
How clean does the toothpick have to be?

Topic Sentence: The first sentence of your paragraph should tell what kind of directions you are giving, but make sure you write a complete sentence. "Baking a cake is easy if you follow these steps." "You can change a flat tire by yourself." "Skinning a deer is complicated, but you can do it if you follow these steps carefully."

Structure/Organization: After the topic sentence, tell the reader what to do, step-by-step. The first step might be to gather the supplies or tools. You can give a list of the supplies or tools that the reader will need. Then tell each step in order until the end. Use transition words like "first," "next," "then," "later," "finally."

Details: Imagine that you are talking to a person who has never done this task before. Write down the words you would say, and be careful not to leave out words such as THE and A. Explain each step clearly so that your reader knows exactly what to do. Try to imagine what questions the reader might ask and answer them in your paragraph. Sometimes you might want to explain the reasons for doing things a certain way.

Thinking of Ideas (Invention) for Your Process Analysis Paragraph

Make a list of things you know how to do. Your list can include things you do at work, in sports or hobbies and things in your everyday life. You can write directions for an adult or for a child. When you start thinking of things a child has never done before, the list can get really long!

> shoot a free throw — child or young teen
> catch a fish — child, teen, or adult
> change a tire on a car — teen or adult
> make a peanut butter and jelly sandwich — child about 5 years old
> bake a cake — teen or adult
> wash dishes — child about 8 years old
> register for classes — adult
> make a Whopper — teen or adult
> balance the cash register — teen or adult

When you choose your topic, think about your audience/reader. Ask yourself, "Who would want to read my paragraph and learn how to do this?"

If you write about how to make a peanut butter and jelly sandwich, you will need to write in a way that a young child can understand. An adult isn't interested in reading that paragraph because an adult already knows how to make the sandwich.

If you write about how to rebuild a transmission, the person who would want to read your paragraph is someone who already has some experience working on cars. You could assume that the reader knows basic information about cars and mechanical tools. You don't have to explain how to open the hood, and you can use terminology without explaining what every word means.

Things to Think About When You Revise

1. Does the topic sentence (first sentence) of your paragraph tell what you will be explaining? Is it written as a complete sentence?

2. Did you give the steps in order?

3. Did you explain each step clearly so that the reader will know exactly what to do?

4. Did think about your reader's age and background knowledge? Did you use words that your reader will understand?

5. Does your last sentence give the paragraph a feeling of conclusion?

Process Analysis Paragraph #1

Audience: seven-year-old child who hasn't washed his hair by himself before

Washing your hair in the sink is easy if you follow these steps. First get the bottle of shampoo and a big towel and put them on the counter next to the kitchen sink. If there are any dirty dishes in the sink, put them onto the counter and rinse the sink out before you wash your hair. When you're ready to start, turn the faucet knobs until the water is warm but not too hot. Lean forward and put your head in the sink under the faucet. Let the water pour over your head until your hair is completely wet. Open the shampoo bottle and squirt some shampoo into the palm of one of your hands. Use a blob of shampoo about the size of a marble. Use your other hand to set the shampoo bottle on the counter so that it won't spill. Use both hands to rub the shampoo all over your head. Then let the water pour over your head until all the shampoo is rinsed away. If your hair is very dirty, you might want to put on the shampoo and rub it around a second time. Be sure to rinse out all the shampoo when you're finished. Then dry your hair with the towel. Now your hair is clean and fresh! Wasn't that easy?

Process Analysis Paragraph #2

Audience: teen or adult who has made a cake from a mix but not from scratch

Baking a cake from scratch is not much harder than using a mix. First make sure you have all the ingredients: flour, sugar, butter, milk, baking powder, salt, vanilla extract, and two eggs. About an hour before you want to start baking, measure 1/4 of a cup of butter and set it out on the counter so that it can warm up to room temperature. The cake will turn out better if the butter is soft. After the butter is room temperature, preheat the oven to 350 degrees. Grease a 9×13 inch pan with vegetable shortening and dust the pan with flour. Measure 1 cup of flour, 2 teaspoons of baking powder, and 1/2 teaspoon of salt into a small bowl. Use a spoon to stir these ingredients together until they are blended. Then take a large bowl and put the softened butter and 3/4 cup of sugar into it. Use your electric beater and beat the butter and sugar on high speed for about 2 minutes until they are completely mixed together. The butter and sugar mixture will be light yellow and fluffy-looking. Now add one egg to the bowl. Beat it into the sugar and butter with the beaters. Then do the same thing with the second egg. Next pour about half of the flour mixture into the large bowl. Beat it together for about 20 seconds, just until it is blended. Pour in 1/4 cup of milk and beat it some more for about 10 seconds. Then add the rest of the flour mixture and beat it for about 20 seconds. Finally pour in another 1/4 cup of milk and beat it one last time just until everything is blended together. You can put away the beater now. Add 1 teaspoon of vanilla extract to the batter and stir it in with a spoon. Use a spatula to scrape all of the batter into the pan. Put the pan in the oven and set the timer for 40 minutes. When the timer rings, test the cake with a toothpick. When the cake is done, the toothpick will come out dry. If there is any wet batter on the toothpick, the cake needs to cook for five more minutes or until the toothpick comes out clean. After the cake cools, you can frost it just like you would frost a cake from a mix. Making a cake from scratch is more work than using a mix, but the cake will taste delicious, and your friends will be very impressed!

Exposition — Proving a Point

When you write an expository paragraph, you prove something to the reader by giving specific information. Write the point that you want to prove as your topic sentence (the first sentence of the paragraph). Then give details and information in the rest of the paragraph to prove that your topic sentence is true.

Topic Sentence: The first sentence of your paragraph should tell the main idea of your paragraph. This is the point that you will prove to your reader. "LeBron James is a stellar basketball player." "My grandma is the keystone of our family." "Disney World is a great place to go on vacation."

Reasons: Your reasons will answer the question "Why?" "Why is Disney World a great place to go on vacation?" After you tell each reason, give specific examples. Imagine that the reader is skeptical and keeps asking you questions:

Topic sentence	You:	Disney World is a great place to go on vacation.
	Reader:	Why? What's so great about Disney World?
Reason #1	You:	There are different kinds of rides.
	Reader:	Like what?
Details for #1	You:	There's Space Mountain if you like roller coasters, Haunted Mansion if you like special effects, and Peter Pan for little kids.
	Reader:	Ok, but is there anything else besides rides?
Reason #2	You:	There are lots of great restaurants.
	Reader:	Like what?
Details for #2	You:	There's King Stefan's Banquet Hall in the upstairs of Cinderella's Castle. Also in Epcot you can eat foods in the different countries like France and Mexico.
	Reader:	What's your favorite food in Disney World?
	You:	The bakery in the France section of Epcot has wonderful treats.
	Reader:	Like what?
	You:	You can get pastries filled with cream, cookies, tarts, and cake.
	Reader:	The rides and food sound really good. Is there anything else that makes Disney World great?
Reason #3	You:	If you like the water, there are lots of fun things to do.
	Reader:	Like what?
Details for #3	You:	All the hotels have nice pools, and there are several water parks with water slides. There's a lake where you can rent a boat or a jet ski.
	Reader:	Ok, you proved it to me. Disney World sounds great.

Structure/Organization: An expository paragraph takes more planning than many other types of paragraphs. One you have decided what reasons you want to tell about, you need to decide what order to put them in. The most important thing is to put similar reasons together. You might want to make a simple outline of your reasons and your examples. An outline is just a list of your information in the order that you will write everything.

> Disney World is a great place to go on vacation.
> > Rides
> > > Space Mountain
> > > Haunted Mansion
> > > Peter Pan
> > Restaurants
> > > King Stefan's Banquet Hall
> > > Mexico
> > > France
> > Water fun
> > > Hotel pools
> > > Water parks
> > > Lake

For more examples and practice with planning your structure and writing outlines, turn to page 100–103. Use transition words like "one," "another," "also," "last," "finally."

Things to Think About When You Revise

1. Does the topic sentence (first sentence) of your paragraph tell the point you will prove?

2. Did you give several reasons to prove your point?

3. Did you give at least one specific detail for each reason?

4. Did think about the order of your reasons and details? Did you put similar things together?

5. Does your last sentence give the paragraph a feeling of conclusion?

There are many different topics you can write about in an expository paragraph.

Stellar

Stellar means *like a star*. For this paragraph, pick a person who is wonderfully talented at what he or she does. You can write about a famous person or someone you know. Pick someone that you already know about. If you have to go online to find out information about the person, you will be doing research, and then you'll either have to use documentation or you'll be plagiarizing. You don't have to know all the details of someone's life in order to prove to your reader that he or she is stellar. You just have to be familiar with that person's work or why he/she is stellar.

Fill in the blanks to create your topic sentence:

_____ is a stellar _____.

> LeBron James is a stellar basketball player.
> Julia Roberts is a stellar actress.
> Elvis was a stellar musician.
> Bobby Bowden was a stellar coach.
> Anne is a stellar boss.

For your reasons and examples, imagine that your reader wants to disagree with you. "Julia Roberts is not all that great. I don't think she is a stellar actress." To convince the reader, you need to tell the reasons why you think she is a stellar actress. Only give information that you already know. Don't look things up on the internet.

Describing a Person

For this paragraph, pick a person you would like to write about and think of the word that describes that person best. You can write about a famous person or someone you know. Pick someone that you already know about. If you have to go online to find out information about the person, you will be doing research, and then you'll either have to use documentation or you'll be plagiarizing. You don't have to know all the details of someone's life in order to write about him or her. You just need to be able to give several examples that prove your point.

Fill in the blanks to create your topic sentence:

_____ is a _____.

> Lady Gaga is a controversial singer.
> Martin Luther King, Jr., was a courageous man.
> George Clooney is a versatile actor.
> Hillary Clinton is a strong woman.
> Christopher Reeve was a hero.

Vacation

This paragraph is fun to write. It's almost like writing a travel guide or advertisement. To think of an idea, make a list of all the places you have lived or visited. Choose your top two places and do a three minute freewrite about each of them. Then choose the place that you think would be most fun to write about. Your topic sentence will be something like this:

_____ is a good place to go on vacation.

When you give your reasons and details, tell things that you already know. Don't look up information on the internet. If you go online to find out information about the place, you will be doing research, and then you'll either have to use documentation or you'll be plagiarizing. You don't have to know all the details about the place you're writing about. Just tell the things that you think make it a good place for a vacation.

Keystone

A *masonry arch* is an arch made out of stones. *Masonry* means stone, brick, or concrete. The ancient Romans used masonry arches in many of their huge buildings and bridges because arches are very strong. To construct the arch, the builders first had to make a wooden framework to hold the stones in place until the very top stone was put in. This top stone was called the *keystone* because it locked all the other stones in place. The keystone held the entire arch together. Once the keystone was in place, the builders could take down the wooden framework and the arch would stand.

A person can be like a keystone too. In many groups of people (family, sports team, club, church, workplace) there is one person who holds everyone else together. The keystone person might be the official leader of the group (team captain or coach, club president, manager) or the keystone might just be a member of the group who has an ability to keep the group working smoothly.

Your topic sentence will be something like this:

My grandma is the keystone of our family.
Brittany is the keystone of the Graham Burger King.

Inspiration

Masonry Arches

Colosseum

Aqueduct

Discovery — Writing to Figure Something Out

In discovery writing, you put your thoughts on paper and discover what you think while writing. There is no right or wrong answer with discovery writing, but you do want to explain why this is the right answer for you. A discovery paragraph can be a story, or it can be several examples or reasons.

Topic Sentence: the first sentence of your paragraph should tell the point or main idea of the paragraph.

Structure/Organization: If your paragraph is a story, structure it like a narrative paragraph using time order. If your paragraph is not a story, structure it like an expository paragraph, telling one reason at a time in a list order.

Details: If your paragraph needs to be longer, imagine your reader is asking you questions: "Why?" "Like what?" "Anything else?" Answering these questions will help you add details to make your paragraph longer and more interesting.

Things to Think About When You Revise

1. Does the topic sentence (first sentence) of your paragraph tell the point or main idea of the paragraph?

2. Did you use a structure that works for your topic? (Time order or List order)

3. What kinds of details did you give so that the reader understands what you mean? Can you add any more details?

4. Do you want to add any dialogue to your paragraph? Dialogue is words that people speak out loud. See page 76 for information on how to write dialogue.

5. Does your last sentence give the paragraph a feeling of conclusion?

Here are some discovery topics.

Your Rock

An ancient Greek myth tells the story of Sisyphus (SIS uh phus). When Sisyphus died, he used a trick to escape from death and live happily for several more years. The second time he died, the Greek gods wanted to make sure he couldn't pull any more tricks. They gave him a huge rock and told him that he had to roll it up a mountain. When Sisyphus finally got to the top, the rock always rolled back down, and Sisyphus had walk down the mountain and roll the rock up again. He had to do this for eternity.

The Greek gods thought that the rock would punish Sisyphus in two ways. One way was that pushing the rock was hard work. This was his physical torture. The second way was that Sisyphus would be miserable doing the same thing over and over. This was his mental torture.

The French philosopher Albert Camus (cam MOO) described it like this: "[When] melancholy rises in man's heart, this is the rock's victory; this is the rock itself." Camus meant that the melancholy was the real torture, not rolling the rock.

What the gods didn't realize was that they could control Sisyphus' body but not his mind. He had to push the rock, but he didn't have to be miserable. He could learn to be happy pushing the rock. By keeping a positive attitude, he was stronger than his rock.

Sisyphus' rock can be compared to many things in the world today. What things do we have to do that seem pointless? What things do we have to do over and over again for eternity (laundry, shaving)? Some people live with very heavy rocks such as serious medical problems. Other rocks could be money troubles or family troubles. Even a 7:00 a.m. class is a rock if you are not a morning person. Some rocks can be fixed; others last forever.

Think about it: what is your rock? How can you be stronger than your rock? Write a paragraph telling what your rock is and how you can be stronger than the rock by either fixing it or by not letting it make you miserable.

Unexpected

In this paragraph, tell what you expected and then tell what actually happened. Your topic sentence will be something like this:

> I got a big surprise the first time I met my girlfriend's parents.
> Having my own apartment was not what I expected.
> I was very nervous about starting college, but now I really enjoy it.

Your paragraph will have two parts. Right after the topic sentence, tell what you expected. Then tell what really happened. Be sure to end with a sentence that gives a feeling of conclusion to the paragraph.

Here are some ideas:

> What did you expect college would be like? What is it really like?
> What did you expect your boyfriend or girlfriend to be like? What is he/she really like?
> What did you expect when you got your first car?
> What did you expect when you started a new job?
> What did you expect when you got married?
> What did you expect when you got your first apartment or roommate?
> What did you expect when you got a new pet?
> What did you expect when you met your in-laws for the first time?

The Genie

Imagine that a genie gave you three wishes. What would you wish for? (You can't wish for more wishes!) Tell the three things one at a time and give plenty of details. Also explain why you would choose each thing. Your topic sentence will be something like this:

> If a genie gave me three wishes, I would wish for a million dollars, a beautiful girlfriend, and a mansion with a swimming pool.

> If a genie gave me three wishes, I would wish for health, love, and world peace.

When you tell the details about your three things, be sure to put them in the same order that you listed them in your topic sentence. End with a sentence that gives the paragraph a feeling of conclusion.

Mr. Clean or Pig Pen

Imagine someone offers to pay you $100,000 if you can go a whole year without washing yourself or brushing your teeth. You don't get the money until the year is up. Would you accept the challenge? If you say yes, explain how you would make it through the year. Think about your job, school, friends, family. If you say no, tell the reasons why you wouldn't do it.

Your topic sentence will be something like this:

> For $100,000 I would definitely go a whole year without washing or brushing my teeth.

Two Roads

Tell about a decision you made or something that happened that changed your life. It could be something good or something bad. Maybe it seemed bad at the time, but it turned out to be good. Maybe it seemed good, but it turned out to be bad. Tell the story of what happened and how it changed your life. Your topic sentence will be something like this:

> When I made a dentist appointment for 9/11/01, I didn't know that this appointment would save my life.

> Marrying my husband was the best decision I ever made.

Inspiration

"The Road Not Taken"
Robert Frost (1874–1963)

Two roads diverged in a yellow wood,
And sorry I could not travel both
And be one traveler, long I stood
And looked down one as far as I could
To where it bent in the undergrowth;

Then took the other, as just as fair,
And having perhaps the better claim,
Because it was grassy and wanted wear;
Though as for that the passing there
Had worn them really about the same,

And both that morning equally lay
In leaves no step had trodden black.
Oh, I kept the first for another day!
Yet knowing how way leads on to way,
I doubted if I should ever come back.

I shall be telling this with a sigh
Somewhere ages and ages hence:
Two roads diverged in a wood, and I —
I took the one less traveled by,
And that has made all the difference.

Excerpt from *Great Expectations* by Charles Dickens:

That was a memorable day to me, for it made great changes in me. But it is the same with any life. Imagine one selected day struck out of it, and think how different its course would have been. Pause you who read this, and think for a moment of the long chain of iron or gold, of thorns or flowers, that would never have bound you, but for the formation of the first link on one memorable day.